A Mother's Touch

ELISE ARNDT

While this book is designed for your personal profit
and enjoyment, it is also intended for group study.
A Leader's Guide with Victor Multiuse Transparen-
cy Masters is available from your local bookstore or
from the publisher.

VICTOR BOOKS ®

A DIVISION OF SCRIPTURE PRESS PUBLICATIONS INC.
USA CANADA ENGLAND

Ninth printing, 1989

Recommended Dewey Decimal Classification: 241
    Suggested Subject Heading: CHILDREN—MANAGEMENT

Library of Congress Catalog Card Number: 82-62219
ISBN: 0-88207-101-7

VICTOR BOOKS
A division of SP Publications, Inc.
        Wheaton, Illinois 60187

Contents

To my mom and dad,

Lydia and Albert Rehberger,

who, because of their Christlike love active in our home,

were used as God's instruments in my life.

1
Baby Birds

The reality of motherhood was magnified for me after the birth of our fourth child, John, in 1970. Warren and I were missionaries in New Guinea, living in a primitive highland village. Having a fourth baby in five years was nothing out of the ordinary there. And yet everything about this birth was unusual for me For although Elisabeth had been born in New Guinea, we were living near other missionaries then and had some of the comforts of home. This time, we would be totally on our own in an unfamiliar setting.

To the New Guineans, a normal delivery is merely a strenuous task performed, for which the mother needs only brief recuperation. Most of the women still have their babies in the bush. American and European women living in New Guinea go to the hospital for the birth. Yet even for them, childbirth is more matter-of-fact than in the United States. After delivery, the new baby is placed in the mother's arms. She is escorted to her room and from that time is in charge of caring for the infant. As I walked from the delivery room with Warren, our three little ones already tugging at me, I felt weary. In the days that followed I kept mulling over the awesome responsibility ahead of me. How was I going to cope with it? Would I be able to meet the needs of my children? No one could have ever prepared me for this experience. It was one which could only be taught as it took place in my life.

We returned to our bush home in the mountains of the Pogera, where I began to learn what the role of Mother was all about, without any modern conveniences or support from people of my own culture. Little did I know that those years spent among the Ipili people would be a most valuable time of learning, for us as a family and for me as a mother.

I look back on those years fondly and consider them my private tutoring in the fine art of mothering. The New Guinean woman was an artist when it came to caring for her children. In that primitive setting I learned many principles which assisted me in rearing happy, secure, and independent children. My natural God-given mothering instinct was encouraged by the people of this primitive culture.

Of course, there were many times when I felt trapped by my circumstances. The mountains surrounding me seemed to block out the rest of the known world. Sometimes the pressures of children who were dependent on just me made me feel like I wanted to run away. But living in the bush gave little opportunity for escape. I was literally bound on all sides. The pressures coming at me were sometimes as great as the mountains were high.

My children's entire world revolved around me. Even though Daddy tried to help out, I was the one they turned to. I was their "comfort station" for runny noses, extra hugs and kisses, skinned knees, and broken toys. I was the one who had nursed them, who sang to them, and read their storybooks. They wanted me in the middle of the night when they had a bad dream or had to go to the bathroom.

I had no modern "luxuries" such as hot running water, a

washer or dryer, telephone or grocery stores, and had only a woodburning stove on which to cook. My circumstances made it extremely difficult to be the perfect Mom I had once envisioned myself becoming.

On one of my really down days, I received a letter from a missionary nurse who had recently visited our outstation. She had observed the close attachment between me and my children. Every time I would move, my four little ones seemed to move with me. It was difficult for them to make up to a stranger, especially if that strange face was white. The black face of the New Guinean was the one with which they felt most secure. In her letter, the nurse expressed a concern that my children's attachment to me might be detrimental to their emotional development.

As if I didn't have enough problems! And now I had a new one to deal with. I had no choice in the matter. My children had no one else to become attached to. There were no grandparents near to take my children for an afternoon, no preschool to send them to, no baby-sitter to leave them with. There was no place I could go to get away from them for even a short period of time. The bathroom was my only place of seclusion, but even there, I would hear little voices outside the door calling: "Mommy, we want to come in."

I began to think that perhaps my friend was right. Maybe my children were too dependent on me. I tried to devise ways we could be separated. A spare room in the back of the house was turned into a playroom, to help them become more independent! But regardless of how comfortable it was, they would carry their toys to the kitchen and play beside me.

My children had many New Guinean playmates, and I would encourage them to play at their friends' houses only to find them returning frequently, just to check to see if I was still home. I don't know where they thought I could have possibly gone. Their father would take them for long walks during which they wanted to go home to see Mommy. "Certainly," they thought, "she must be lonely for us." I was faced with a dilemma. How would I ever get my children to become independent of me?

Wasoanda's Wisdom

In my frustration I began to observe the Ipili women and their children. They never had the opportunity to hear a psychologist speak about rearing emotionally strong children. Yet, I saw in them an instinctive knowledge of how to mother their children to independence.

My children's attachment to me was mild compared to the attachment between a New Guinean child and his mother. Rarely separated from their mothers, these children were either sleeping in net bags on their mothers' backs, sitting on their mothers' shoulders, or in their mothers' arms, nursing.

Babies were allowed to nurse until they weaned themselves—up to four years of age. When a mother worked in her garden, her baby was close by. At the first sounds of crying, the mother would stop her work and minister the love necessary to soothe her child. A fretful baby meant something was wrong. Very seldom would I hear a baby cry for long periods of time. It was believed that a crying baby meant an unhappy or sick baby. "Don't let your baby cry," they would tell me. "He will get a headache, even get sick, and possibly die." To allow a baby to cry for any length of time was considered cruel.

Work stopped when a baby wanted to be fed. It was a welcome interruption for the mother who needed rest from the hard work she was doing in her garden. She would caress her baby's skin while she nursed him, speaking to him in soft loving tones. It was an enjoyable time for both of them.

These children were extremely dependent on their mothers for security, love, and physical contact, and were not even separated from them at night while they slept. As I observed the Ipili families, I began to realize that this dependence of the children on the mothers, especially within the first six years of life, was considered necessary in order to produce secure children.

As the children grew into adolescence, they became independent, loving, successful members of the society. The dependence during the formative years actually seemed to produce independence later.

Children were considered babies until they lost their front teeth. When this happened, the little boys of the tribe left their mothers and went to live with the men in the village. Fathers then took over the nurturing of their sons and the mothers raised the girls.

We had adopted an elderly Ipili woman, Wasoanda, as grandmother to our children. Wasoanda was dismayed when I told her I wanted to make my children more independent of me. She could not understand why such a thought should even enter my mind. To keep a baby close to his mother was the way it was supposed to be. Anything else was cruel and unnatural.

With beautiful simplicity, she spoke words of wisdom which I will never forget. I have used them to encourage other mothers who are struggling with clinging children.

"Missus," Wasoanda said, "don't try to make your children go away from you. They are too little yet to do that. Your babies need you. They are like baby birds. Keep them close to you like a mother bird keeps her baby birds under her wings. When your children lose their front teeth, they will sprout their wings and fly away."

Wasoanda knew nothing about American culture. She didn't know that children left their mothers at age five or six and embarked on a new adventure called kindergarten, or that during that year many children would lose their first teeth.

Wasoanda was saying that my children needed the security of the nest. Eventually they would all leave. But what they needed now, and until that great event of losing their front teeth took place, was the closeness which only a mother could provide.

Instinctive Mothering

Today some psychologists and pediatricians are urging the rediscovery of good mothering, especially within the early years of a child's life. For somehow, within the past two generations, this instinctive type of mothering was replaced with the philosophy that children must grow up quickly and be prepared to leave their mothers at an early age. As a result, Mother is no longer considered to be the primary influence in a child's life. She is being replaced by day-care centers, baby-sitters, and sophisticated nursery programs designed to make a toddler a well-adjusted member of society.

Our grandmothers would be appalled at modern attitudes about rearing children. They could not have explained their childrearing techniques with any type of scientific rationale. They only practiced something which they felt inside. Mothering was instinctive, and was encouraged by other people in the community. Our grandmothers did not know what was best, scientifically or emotionally. They just did what seemed the natural thing and found it satisfying.

Grandmother would be surprised today to hear the simple things she did with her baby described by psychologists in such scientific terms as tactile and kinesthetic stimulation, mutual gaze patterns, visual stimulus of the mother's face, auditory feedback, and differential stimuli for smiling. She would describe it as,

- "Love begins in the mother's arms."
- "Talk to your baby as much as possible."
- "Touch, love, and kiss him as often as you like."
- "Don't be afraid of spoiling him."
- "Don't let your baby cry. He needs you and that's his way of telling you to come to him. He cries for a reason."

Grandmother knew all along that her tiny baby was smiling in response to her voice, and discounted the doctor's opinion that it was just a "gas smile."

Her attitudes toward mothering, and the importance of the bonding between her and her child, was something which wasn't even questioned. It was just supposed to be that way. Because it was natural, under favorable conditions it led to the establishment of stable and lasting bonds of love which carried over into the adult life of her child.

This is quite a contrast to the insecurity so many modern mothers feel about their role. And this insecurity is being fostered by the media and societal agitators. Mother is no longer considered the primary influence for raising healthy, happy, secure children. Day-care centers, nursery schools, and baby-sitters supposedly know more about rearing children than Mother. Something which is so instinctive is being discouraged.

Much of society says that Grandmother's ways are really primitive and obsolete. Yet psychologists are reevaluating this instinctive knowledge. Many doctors and experts in childrearing are speaking out loudly and boldly about getting Mother back into the home, so that those bonds of love between Mother and child become more firmly established.

The first years of a child's life can never be stressed enough. To treat them casually can mean emotional disaster later in the child's life. Improper attitudes toward mothering may produce children with intellectual deficits, emotional problems, and an inability to love and form lasting relationships. Many teenagers today fit into the last category. They are starved for affection, are restless, and sense no direction or purpose in their lives. Some try to fill that void with rebellion to authority, drugs, sex, and a general attitude of complacency.

In his book, *How To Really Love Your Teenager,* Dr. Ross Campbell says:

Far too many teenagers today feel that no one really cares about them. As a result, many of them have feelings of worthlessness, hopelessness, helplessness, poor self-esteem, and self-depreciation.

Today's teenagers are described by many as the "apathetic generation." Why is this? Because so many teens see themselves in a negative way, as unappreciated and worthless. Such a self-concept is the natural result of a child not feeling genuinely loved and cared for.

Two of the most frightening results of this apathy are depression and revolt against authority. Apathetic teens can become easy prey for unscrupulous persons who use young people for their own ends. They are susceptible to being influenced by authoritarian groups that provide easy answers and impossible promises (Victor Books, p. 9).

A Mother's Decision

It is so important for a young child to experience a warm, intimate, and continuing relationship with his mother. Even brief separation from the mother, and from the quality of the mother's relationship with her child, can profoundly affect the child's physical and emotional development.

In her book *Every Child's Birthright: In Defense of Mothering*, Selma Fraiberg cautions about the effects improper mothering will have on the coming generation:

We are seeing a devaluation of parental nurturing and commitment to babies in our society which may affect the quality and stability of the child's human attachments in ways that cannot yet be predicted.

A baby who is stored like a package with neighbors and relatives while his mother works may come to know as many different caretakers as a baby in the lowest grade institution, and at the age of one or two years, can resemble in all significant ways the emotionally deprived babies of such an institution (Preface x, xii, p. 54).

Proper mothering is not the cure-all for family problems, for there are many other factors which influence the growth of children. But it is the answer to some of them. Parents who give children the proper emotional and spiritual foundation in the early years will prevent much heartache later. We have the responsibility to provide all the love and care our children need so that they can grow into mature adults, able to cope with life.

In the Bible we read, "Train up a child in the way he should go, even when he is old he will not depart from it" (Proverbs 22:6). Those early years of a child's life mold and shape his character more than any other period of time.

A boy criminal who shocked the world several years ago by committing a series of senseless murders with a pistol, wrote a diary in prison. He said in it: "I hear that one's personality and character are formed by the time one is five years old. Five years in man's lifetime is only a short time (a few years and months). But if it forms a character which influences his whole life to this degree, what important years they are, and how negligent parents are." (Masaru Ibuka, *Kindergarten Is Too Late*, Simon and Schuster, p. 22).

Within the past 40 years the work force of women has increased dramatically. In 1910, 20 percent of the U.S. labor force was women; now, the figure is close to 50 percent.

The following statistics, released by the Urban Institute, Washington, D.C., appeared in an article published by *Nation's Business*, November 1979:

By 1990, more than 55 percent of all women age 16 and up will be in the work force.

Urban Institute statistics show that by 1990: 52 million women will be working or looking for work, including two-thirds of all married women under 55 and more than half of the mothers with children under the age of six; women will be entering the work force at a rate of 1 million more working women than in 1947; and, only 25 percent of all women will be full-time homemakers (p. 33).

Redbook (October 1980) stated this fact:

More than 50 percent of women in the United States today with children under the age of three are working presumably because of need of their own (either to provide income or to provide necessary outlets for themselves). In these families the small, vulnerable children may be left in care situations that are totally inadequate (p. 115).

Mothers today face a dilemma: Should we join the work force and be part of the 50 percent of women who leave small children at home? Or should we be full-time moms?

The decision to work or not to work is a difficult one, especially since we are living in such stressful economic times. Inflation is a serious matter in the life of a family, and it is increasingly more difficult to make ends meet, especially as a family grows.

For a mother not to work means sacrifice. It may mean doing without things, while others around us seemingly prosper. New carpeting, furniture, or a second car are pretty important in some women's lives.

For a mother to work, to provide for a better physical life, also means sacrifice. It will mean having to give up precious moments with our children which we will never be able to recapture. It may involve risking problems later, if that seemingly independent toddler grows into a teenager who is dependent on stimulants or the wrong kinds of relationships to fill the emotional void.

I know there are situations in which it is necessary for a mother of small children to work. If a woman is the sole provider for the family, she works not to fulfill her own needs, or to buy extras, but because she has to. If given a choice she would probably prefer to stay at home. I believe that God gives a special grace and wisdom to these mothers, and that He will keep their children in His care.

If you feel pressured into finding full-time employment outside your home, you may want to evaluate your reasons for working. You might also take a look ahead to the future, to determine the cost of your decision. Is working now worth the risk? Can you wait until your children are older?

"It has been estimated that if a woman of 25 with two children, two years apart, gives full time to rearing them until they are 18, it leaves her with still two-thirds of her adult life to follow whatever interest she desires" (*Pastoral Renewal,* p. 19, May 1980). I have seen many women pursue careers later in life, and achieve satisfying levels of success.

Character Formation

To insure the emotional bonding that needs to take place, young children need as much physical touch and love from Mother as possible. Some people say that anyone can do the job of mothering, and it is true that anyone can take care of the physical necessities of children. But physical care is only a small part of the total picture. The job of mothering goes far beyond feeding the children, washing their clothes, picking up toys, or changing dirty diapers.

Into this daily routine comes the formation of character. As the mother interacts with them on a physical level, and relates to them on emotional, intellectual, and spiritual levels, children learn what it means to be a part of a community called the family. They learn attitudes about life. They form ideas of God and of what the love of Jesus is like. They learn how to love and be loved. They begin to see the difference between what is acceptable behavior and what is not, between what is right and what is wrong.

Anyone can be paid to do the physical work of rearing children, but only Mother can daily add the other dimensions. This is what makes her role so special to the total life experience of her children.

Every child has the right to this type of love from his mother. My heart aches when I see physically abused children. And yet, little is said about children who are in a state of severe emotional and spiritual privation because of an absent mother.

Mother is usually the one who provides the proper environment for the Holy Spirit to work on the tender heart of the child. Therefore, we should never look on full-time mothering as something insignificant. We need to be serious about our calling and not shrug it off as a job anyone else could do as well.

A Mother's Reward

Mothers of young children need much encouragement. The job they perform is often a thankless one. They feel weighed down with responsibility, and may wonder if they even have a personal identity. In one of my down times when all my children were small, I said to my husband, "I don't even feel like a person. All I do is nurse babies, and change dirty diapers."

Maybe you feel that way at times. It's very common to question your own identity during the early years of childrearing. But as one who has been there, I can promise you that it is worth every minute of the seeming captivity.

My four demanding, dependent baby birds are now teenagers. They have sprouted their wings and are flying away, one by one, because they are secure enough to do so. I have loved and held them close all these years, and in so doing I have prepared them to be able to give of that love to a world which needs it so desperately.

We go places as a family, laugh and play together, plan and worship together. We are experiencing a marvelous time as a family, and I thank God for those important early years that prepared us for the reward we now see.

Wasoanda's advice to me has paid off. There will be plenty of time for me to do all the things God would have me do. I must be patient. All the great deeds I might accomplish in my life could never equal the privilege of raising four precious children for God.

Keep your baby birds close to you—the closer the better. God will give you the ability and grace to cope. All too soon your babies will fly out of the nest, and you will be proud that you have had a vital part in the formation of their character.

It might seem easier to let someone else raise your children. But if you do, it will eventually take its toll on your family. Do the job to which God has called you. The blessings will far outnumber the frustrations, as you see your children grow into all that God wants them to be.

2
Loaned, Not Owned

When death comes to a child, we ask why. When it happens in a family who is dear to us, we internalize the pain and go through the grief process as though it were our own child. Our human nature rebels against giving up ownership of our children to anyone, even to God who rightfully owns them.

It was during the Christmas season of 1978 that I once again had to deal with the matter of who owned my children. Within less than 16 hours, two families in our congregation lost a child.

John was soon to graduate from high school and was beginning to see direction in his life. One cold winter day, as he was working on his new car in a closed garage, he was overcome by carbon monoxide fumes, and soon died. Sixteen hours later, 13-year-old Eddie was killed on a school playground when a gust of wind caused a small building to collapse and fall on him.

As their pastor, Warren bore primary responsibility for bringing Christian comfort to the families, and for planning the two funerals. As their friends and fellow members of the body of Christ, we felt devastated by such great losses, and cried out, "Why, God? Why all the hurt? Why at such a young age? Why to people we love? To people who love You?"

As a mother of four children, I projected all of this on my own family. What if it had been my Paul or David on that playground? What if Warren and I were making funeral arrangements? How would I be reacting? Would I be able to cope with losing one of my children?

I began to pray, "Lord, please don't ever put me through that type of testing. I know I wouldn't be able to endure." In my humanness, I couldn't even think of the possibility of losing one of my children, of giving up my ownership.

In my grief I knew there was one person who would understand how I felt. When I called my mother long distance, she sensed right away that something was wrong. I began to pour out the ache in my heart, the grief I was experiencing, but also the fear I had of losing one of my children. "Mom, two boys in our congregation were just killed. Mom, how could that happen? I'm so afraid of losing my own children. Why is there so much pain and sorrow? Why does God allow such things to happen, especially to people who love Him?"

In her quiet, beautiful, God-fearing way, she spoke words to me which have influenced my thinking about my children.

"Elise, our children have been only loaned to us. They are God's special blessings to us, but we cannot claim ownership. They belong to Him. When He desires to call them home, we must be ready to release them, knowing we have done our best to prepare them for that time."

It hit me hard—"Loaned, not owned." God did grant me ownership in a physical way, since I was the one to give birth to them. But true ownership of my children really belongs to Him.

Yet, to think that my children were not really mine seemed unreasonable. After all, my body provided the proper nourishment for their growth. I had nursed my children at my breast and had stayed up many nights caring for them when they were ill. They were my flesh and blood, a very part of me. If I would lose one of them, surely it would be like losing a part of myself. I loved my children too much to even consider the fact that someday they might be taken from me.

A Test of Faith

On that grief-filled day, memories flooded into my mind of the years Warren and I spent in New Guinea. It seemed so distant and yet, so very close and real at this time. Johnny had just been born, and was welcomed royally by his two brothers and his sister who were waiting for me after delivery to greet him. Their curiosity was at a peak as I unwrapped Johnny's blankets and let them touch his soft skin. They counted on each hand and foot to make sure he had enough fingers and toes. They kissed and cuddled him and unanimously decided that he would be an acceptable member of our family. He had passed their test.

It was amazing to me how quickly we learned to love John. He was not yet 60 minutes old, and he belonged to us. The love in that hospital room filled our family with an even deeper love for each other. We named our little boy John because it means "Gracious Gift of God."

John was four weeks old when we returned to our outstation home in the Pogera of New Guinea. We were anxious to settle into a normal routine once again. Our four little ones needed their own beds and toys, and Warren needed to get back to his assigned work. John seemed to be doing well on leaving the hospital, but two days after our return home, he developed bronchial pneumonia. I began to see the same symptoms developing in John that I had seen in many of the New Guinean babies who had recently died from pneumonia. His temperature soared, he was listless, and his breathing became labored. When he refused to nurse or respond to my voice, I knew that he was very seriously ill.

Panic-stricken at the possibility of losing him, we called the hospital via two-way radio asking if they could provide any type of assistance. We needed to get John back to the hospital. It was evening and no helicopter would be able to evacuate us until the next morning. By that time it might be too late. A feeling of complete helplessness came over me. I was sure I was going to lose my baby; nothing I was able to do would stop it from happening. No help was available—no doctors, no hospitals, no medicine. Only God could intervene. My husband and I prayed until we couldn't pray any longer. Our faith was at its lowest as we struggled with God: "Lord, You cannot take our little John now. We haven't had a chance to see him grow up. Even at four weeks we love him so much. He is part of us. He is *ours.*" John continued to struggle with every breath he took and we wrestled with the thought of his death.

The New Guinean elders came to our spiritual rescue that night. We had given up even trying to convince God. When Warren and I could no longer pray, the elders prayed for a miracle and believed God would see us through. In my weary state, I took John into my arms and there released him to the Lord. "He is not mine, Lord." I could hardly believe I was saying that. "He's Yours to do with as You please. We have loved him for this short time. I give him up to You."

I cried, but instead of feeling hurt or angry, I felt a sense of relief. Peace flooded my heart as I held John close to me, expecting the Lord to take him at any moment. I was all done fighting for my parental rights to him. As I rocked him in my arms, I closed my eyes and fell into a deep sleep.

No more than an hour had passed when I opened my eyes. John was still breathing. Outside my kitchen window was the most beautiful sunrise I had ever seen. It reminded me of what the psalmist said, "Weeping may last for the night, but a shout of joy comes in the morning" (Psalm 30:5). Along with the sunrise that greeted me, I heard the Lord speaking to me, "Elise, it is going to be all right. John will live! You have surrendered your will to Mine; and I, in My grace, have given John back to you."

I felt like Abraham must have felt after God had told him to offer his only son, Isaac, on the altar. Abraham submitted to the will of God, and then Isaac's life was spared. God had provided a way out for us also, but only after putting us through the testing of our faith.

That morning a helicopter was sent to our isolated mission station. Our family was flown to the mission hospital where John received medical treatment. He made it! God spared his little life. "For this boy I prayed, and the Lord has given me my petition which I asked of Him. So I have also dedicated him to the Lord; as long as he lives he is dedicated to the Lord" (1 Samuel 1:27–28).

A Mother's Submission

This was the experience that passed through my mind when my mother spoke about our children being loaned to us. God had taught me this years ago, and yet I had forgotten. It took the words of my mother to remind me once again: "Elise, your children are only loaned to you. Don't you remember how I used to send you off to school each morning? 'God be with you today and keep you,' I would say."

As a child, I heard these words but never really understood what was behind them. They were a regular part of my day. What I didn't realize until now is that with the blessing came a silent prayer from my mother's heart: "Lord, protect my little ones from harm and danger today; but if this should be the day You choose to take them home, I am willing to give them up to You. I do not own them, for they are Yours and they have only been loaned to me by You. If You choose to grant them another day with me, help me to do all I can to prepare them for the day when You will call them home."

What a prayer of faith! What an attitude of humility and willingness to be in submission to the will of God, laying her ownership of us aside so that we could receive God's best in our lives.

I often think of Mary, the mother of Jesus. She must have experienced some of the same struggles we do. Jesus was given to her, but she did not own Him. This was explained to her from the very beginning. He was to be called the Son of God, not "Mary's boy." Since He was also her firstborn son, according to Levitical law He was to be dedicated or given back to God for service. Mary knew she would someday have to give Him up. Even though she carried Him in her womb, nursed Him at her breast, loved Him as her own, she would have to surrender Him to the will of His heavenly Father.

At eight days of age, Jesus was brought to the temple by His parents. Simeon, a righteous and devout man, was led of the Spirit to the temple on that day. When he looked at Jesus, Simeon knew immediately that this was the promised Messiah (Luke 2:33). Mary and Joseph were amazed at the things which Simeon said about Him. Simeon blessed them and said to Mary: "Behold, this Child is appointed for the fall and rise of many in Israel, and for a sign to be opposed—and a sword will pierce even your own soul" (Luke 2:34–35).

Mary was shown that being a mother was going to hurt her deeply. This Child she loved would be a source of pain in her life. She knew her Son would experience an early death, and the natural emotions of being a mother caused her to feel a sense of grief. Luke 2:51 shows how Mary dealt with this revelation: "And His mother treasured all these things in her heart."

Even though she would give up her ownership of Jesus, she realized she had an important job to do. She and Joseph were to train this little Boy in the things of God, to teach Him everything a young Jewish boy should know, and to prepare Him for the time of His death.

It says in the Scriptures that Jesus continued in subjection to His parents. He needed training and guidance to influence and form His human character. Even though He was true God, He was also true man with a fully human side to His life. Jesus had to learn obedience. "Although He was a Son, He learned obedience from the things which He suffered" (Hebrews 5:8). Jesus needed to be trained, and God chose Mary for that responsibility and privilege.

No Place for Procrastination

My attitudes have changed greatly since that conversation with my mother. The importance of raising my children for Christ came to be much more in my thoughts and priorities. I realized that the time was short, that there was no place for procrastination in relating the things of God to my children. Teaching them about God was going to be a priority in my life. I also began to see that the most effective teaching instrument God wanted me to use was my own life, being lived each day in relationship to Him. I was an example for my children. What they saw lived out on a day-by-day basis in my own life would influence them, both physically and spiritually. I wanted to live a pure life before the Lord and my family. I wanted them to witness Jesus being the very center of my life. My prayer began to be, "Lord, help me to do everything possible to prepare them to meet You."

Sending my children off to school in the morning has become one of my special times. Early in the morning we gather together around the Scriptures, looking to see what the Holy Spirit would want us to learn for the day. Sometimes it is only one verse which we read, but it is a verse that I pray will guide them throughout their day. We commit our day to Jesus. We ask for the protection of His angels around us. We ask the Holy Spirit to make us the light of Jesus to a dark and lonely world. A gentle kiss on the cheek and a warm hug with a "God be with you" send them out the door. I feel I have prepared them for the world outside our home.

And deep in my heart I pray the prayer my mother so often prayed for us: "Lord, help me this day to live my life according to Your will. Help me, by Your Holy Spirit's power within me, to do everything possible to prepare my children for a life of service to You and for eternity. I surrender them to You and to Your keeping, knowing that Your love for them is greater than mine could ever be."

3
Just a Mom

Some years ago, I attended a luncheon at which many professional women were present. They were all dressed in the latest fashion. Their conversations ranged from the problems they were having with baby-sitters for their children to the latest on-the-job experience. It all seemed so glamorous—meetings to attend, expense accounts, recognition for a job well done. Inside I felt a stirring of envy. My days were filled with little children—seeing to it that they behaved properly, ate the right things, wore clean clothes, and received their daily minimum requirement of hugs. My days usually left me exhausted, many times wondering if anything of value was accomplished. Somehow, as I looked around at the luncheon guests, I could not identify with them. They seemed to be concerned about more crucial matters than I was.

I found myself included in a conversation that started off with polite small talk and then progressed to finding out about each other.

A dignified and stunning woman across the table asked, "Elise, what type of work do you do?" At first I was flattered. She hadn't seen through my disguise, assuming that I was a professional woman like the others. But then it dawned on me that I was going to have to do some quick thinking to answer her pointed question.

Should I reply that *I did work* and that my profession by choice was "motherhood"? Would she understand the decision I had made many years ago to be a stay-at-home Mom? Or that I was working hard and long hours at my chosen profession? Would she be able to comprehend that full-time mothering was just as time-consuming, challenging, and productive as her career?

I tried to think up some cute title for the job I performed every day. But titles such as "domestic engineer" or "professional homemaker" just didn't seem adequate. And so, with very little dignity I replied, "No, I don't work. I'm just a mom."

Why was I so ashamed to admit that I was a mother by choice? Was it because I was afraid that anyone who chose to be around kids all day didn't have much to offer the world? Was I beginning to wonder if I had made the wrong decision somewhere along the way? Did I feel threatened by the glamour associated with the professions of the women around me? My job of mothering was minimized that afternoon because I felt insignificant in my choice of profession. Maybe what I was doing wasn't as important as I thought it was.

The pointed question asked that day started me thinking about my importance as a Mom. I was being challenged and I was on the defensive. Yet, I knew it was essential for me to reevaluate why I had chosen motherhood as my profession.

• Why did I put so much emphasis on this common, ordinary task which millions of women perform daily, without any recognition or financial gain?

• Why did I feel so threatened and confused?

• Why was I even feeling guilty about not using my education in a profession outside my home?

- Would my husband and children be more proud of me if I had an outside job?
- Would I be a more confident and productive person?

It didn't take me long to answer the questions about my family. They did not identify with the many doubts I was experiencing. When I announced to them that it was time for me to start thinking about finding some type of work, a look of horror came over their faces. Johnny and Elisabeth's first reaction was: "Who will wake us up in the morning and get us ready for school? Who will fix us breakfast?" Paul and David were next in line: "Mom, does that mean you won't be here when we get home from school? Who will let us in the house?" Now *they* felt threatened: "How will Mom be able to work and still give us all the special attention we need?"

In the weeks that followed, I discovered that my children needed me in the morning not just to wake them up, but to sing to them as I did. They enjoyed the cuddling which accompanied the morning ritual of back rubbing and teasing about being such sleepyheads. They needed me not just to make their lunches but also to go over their spelling words, assuring them that they could get an "A" on the next test if they studied hard enough. They needed me to talk to them and sometimes cuddle with them for a short while before they faced another school day. If I would work, I would miss those precious times of fellowship we enjoyed as a family around God's Word each morning. I would miss my children's enthusiastic entrance into the house at 4 P.M., all trying to tell me what had taken place that day.

I could see I didn't want anyone else taking over my job. I was protective of my position within my home and didn't want anyone else mothering my children.

I had to reevaluate my feelings about being just a mom. I was not merely the "chief cook and bottle washer" of our home. My duties were complex and varied. I found that there were 80 tasks I performed as a housewife to keep my home running smoothly. My daily routine consisted of such duties as chauffeur, secretary, nurse, teacher, mechanic, plumber, C.P.A., interior decorator, seamstress, cook, maid, and psychologist (to name only a few). It was estimated that in 1981 the average house-wife would receive a salary of $793.79 per week or $41,000 per year if she were reimbursed for all the physical services she performs.

That figure does not include all those little extras a mother does for her family, the hugs and kisses, the reading of story-books, and playing house, the comfort which is given in times of crisis, and the joy shared when finally a two-year-old is potty-trained, or a six-year-old loses his first tooth. Those are things which no amount of money can buy.

I came to the conclusion that Mom is one of the most impor-tant elements within any home. She is the one who sets the tone and creates the atmosphere. Home can be the very dwelling place of God, where the love of Jesus is experienced at every turn. Home can be a refuge for a weary husband and uptight children who seek retreat from a world which is really Satan's domain. What a beautiful experience for any child to have a home filled with love, kindness, and joy. When a mother is content in her calling of motherhood and at peace with God, she reflects these attitudes to her family.

No amount of wealth can ever take the place of an absent mother. A child deprived of mother's love, especially within the early childhood years, may show psychoneuroses and character disorders later in life. This is true not only of children who are abandoned as infants but of children who are left in day-care centers, nurseries, and with baby-sitters for prolonged periods of time. You need to seriously consider the effects your absence may eventually have on your children, especially as they enter the teenage years of life.

One of the primary things your young child needs from you is your time. He needs you to interact with him. He needs you to train, discipline, teach, and relate the love of Jesus to him. An absent mother cannot effectively accomplish these things which are so needed to grow loving, independent, secure children.

The Desert Years

You may be in the position right now where you feel you are giving up your rights—your rights to become someone, to prove your abilities. Being called "just a mom" is really being labeled a servant. You are emptied of all the prestige of being someone who matters in the scheme of things in society. And that may seem a form of "humiliation."

I call the early years of mothering the "desert years," when the mother moves from the glamour of being "someone" to the drudgery of housework and screaming kids. It could be that you are a college graduate with a degree behind your name. Maybe you had a high-paying job before your children were born. You were admired and respected by others for your ability in your profession. You were free to buy the type of clothes you liked, free to eat out several times a week, free to come and go as you pleased. Now you are tied down with small children. Not much praise comes your way. No one pats you on the back for staying up all night with a sick child or for washing diapers. The money that used to purchase new clothes now goes to buy new shoes for the children. Even that much-needed winter coat gets pushed out of possibility because of dentist bills.

We tend to forget that each person whom God chooses to use usually has to go through some type of desert experience. Paul (Galatians 1:15—2:1), Moses (Acts 7:40), John the Baptist (Luke 1:80), and even Jesus, God's very own Son (Luke 4:1), had to experience this period in their lives.

The desert experience is a special time God uses in our lives to prepare us for something which He wants us to do later. Because those stay-at-home years are difficult for a mother, and sometimes seem like a waste of time, a feeling of unfulfillment hangs over the heads of many women during that time. But God is at work, teaching us and preparing us for something even greater.

Right now, with children demanding every minute of your time, this may be hard for you to imagine. You will not always be a mother of small children. Soon those years will be behind you and you will be free from the responsibility of caring for dependent, clinging children.

Those desert years were valuable ones for me, for through them, God taught me much about living the Christian life. He drew me away from the world and placed me in seclusion to learn from Him. During those years I learned how to pray, read my Bible, and listen to Him speak to me. I learned how to trust God for each day's problems, to have self-control when I was tempted to scream and yell at my children, and to show gentleness and kindness when the situation around me was anything but gentle and kind. I was schooled in the fine art of servanthood, of dying to self and allowing Jesus to reign within me. I was taught what Philippians 2:3–5 really means in the life of a Christian.

Do nothing from selfishness or empty conceit, but with humility of mind let each of you regard one another as more important than himself; do not merely look out for your own personal interests, but also for the interests of others.

Called From the Kitchen

I thought my desert years would never end. But now, my children are taking responsibility within our home. They help with laundry, ironing, cleaning the house, and cooking, giving me more freedom for ministry with women.

No matter what I may ever do in this world, I will always remain just a Mom to them. That really doesn't upset me anymore. Being their Mom entitles me to the right and privilege of being one of the most vital elements in their physical, emotional, and spiritual development. No one else can do my job better. It has been a job which, by the grace of God, has been done well and has brought dividends and blessings already evident in the life of our family.

Several years ago I was asked to lead a workshop at a conference. Some 2,000 people were expected to attend. I felt honored and delighted, but my children could not understand why I was chosen. They were even more confused when a publication advertising the conference featured their mother's picture on the front page. The caption under the picture said "Elise Arndt, wife of Rev. Warren Arndt, and mother of four children." All the other speakers had distinguished titles—Ph.D., M.A., B.D. Some were professors and pastors. My only significant credential was "pastor's wife and mom."

My children found it difficult to believe their mother had actually made the front page of a newspaper, and asked me, "Mom, why is your picture in this newspaper? You are just our mom and not a speaker like those people." This bothered me until God spoke to me through His Word, as my husband preached a sermon entitled "God Can Use Nobodies" based on 1 Corinthians 1:26–29.

For consider your calling, brethren, that there were not many wise according to the flesh, not many mighty, not many noble; but God has chosen the foolish things of the world to shame the wise, and God has chosen the weak things of the world to shame the things which are strong, and the base things of the world and the despised, God has chosen, the things that are not ... that no man should boast before God.

It was not my credential which made me important to God, but what He was working in and through me. I had been called from my kitchen sink to serve Jesus, and I was not to worry about not having a title, because God's calling was enough.

I went to that conference and was obedient to the Lord in what He wanted me to do. Sure, I was just a Mom, but one who was called by God.

I have learned over the years to proclaim proudly that I am by choice a wife and mother first. Any other titles are of secondary importance.

4
Oatmeal and the Morning Star

The digital alarm clock read 5:56 A.M. as I rolled over to shut it off. Was my day really to begin this early? After all, the sun wasn't even up.

I was trying to convince myself—only to remember that it was no longer summer and sleeping in was a thing of the past. With the start of a new school year came the discipline of rising earlier. Alarm clocks, the sound of water running in the shower, and the buzzing of hair dryers were now the indications that the day was beginning. What a contrast from the lazy summer routine we had all enjoyed.

Still debating if my getting up was really of benefit to anyone, I thought of Hebrews 12:11:

All discipline for the moment seems not to be joyful but sorrowful; yet to those who have been trained by it afterward it yields the peaceful fruit of righteousness. Therefore, strengthen the hands that are weak and the knees that are feeble.

This discipline certainly was not a joyful one and my hands and feet were weak and feeble at that hour. Maybe someday I would see the "peaceful fruit of righteousness" produced in my life because of my obedience to God and what He wanted for me as a mother. But, for now, it was strictly an act of obedience.

An icy cold, linoleum floor was waiting to greet my bare feet. I shivered and then quickly moved to the stove where I began to make a much-needed cup of hot coffee.

A light snow had fallen during the night, and there was frost on the window above my kitchen sink. Even the bright, flowered wallpaper in my kitchen did not help create the glow of warmth I needed. "Only the rising of the morning sun," I thought, "could accomplish that."

This particular fall morning of 1980 was going to be a special one for me, a morning in which I would see the result of many hours and many years of taking time to speak the Word of God to my children. It was going to show me that the time I had invested in the early years of their lives had been blessed.

While the coffee brewed, I began to fill a saucepan with water. Oatmeal was in order for breakfast.

The sound of a large truck, stopping and starting, jolted me into awareness. It was garbage day and our garbage had not been placed on our front curb the night before our collection. The truck was close by, and I knew it would soon be at our house.

"Quick!" I told the boys. "The garbage needs to be put on the curb." A few grumbles and complaints issued forth, while they put on their coats and ran to the garage to carry the plastic bags to the curb.

The water began to boil on the stove just as Paul and David came rushing into the house, filled with excitement.

"Mom, you have to come outside right away. There is something up in the sky we want you to see. It's brighter than anything we have ever seen before." Of course, my imagination began to run away with me. Was it a flying saucer or an unidentified object in the sky?

With my robe wrapped snugly around me, I rushed out the front door, and looked into the eastern sky. There was something wondrous to behold. Hanging in all its splendor was the biggest and brightest star I had ever seen.

It was a glorious sight, a brilliant diamond lying against the backdrop of a black velvet cloth, its radiance breaking through the darkness. I went back into my kitchen and scraped the frost from my window to view with awe the beauty of that "morning star."

Did God, who created the entire universe, want me to learn a new lesson that morning? Was this the blessing He was bestowing on me for my obedience in rising early with my children? Was He trying to reassure me that the morning can be a time of pleasant surprises, an opportunity for praising Him for His creation?

As my children sat down to their oatmeal, I picked up my Bible. I knew that Jesus was referred to as the "bright morning star" in the Scriptures, and I turned to Revelation 22:16, to read the verse to the children: "I, Jesus, have sent My angel to testify to you these things for the churches. I am the root and the offspring of David, the bright morning star."

I was excited about what I had read, but the children's response at first was one of seeming disinterest. They were more engrossed in eating their oatmeal than in my enthusiasm. I persisted, though, and soon they began to listen as I related the events of the morning to our life with God and His Word.

"Did you know," I asked them, "that the star you saw is called the morning star?" Their response was still cautious.

Several days previous I had heard a report on the radio about the morning star and now tried to explain it to them. "Each year the morning star appears in the eastern sky about this time. It is really the Planet Venus. In the summer months it is called the evening star and appears in the west. Some people believe this is the bright star that led the wise men to the Baby Jesus."

At that, their ears perked up a little to see what else would be said. We talked informally for awhile.

"Jesus is our 'Morning Star,'" I said. "He begins our day with His brilliance. His coming into our lives fills all the dark corners of our lives with His light. He gives us the light of His forgiveness and salvation. Just as the morning star shines so brightly because the sky is so black, so the light of Jesus becomes more brilliant in us during the dark moments in our lives."

That morning in our prayers, we prayed for the light of Jesus to shine in our lives as bright as the morning star shines in the dark sky. This definitely was a happening, one which was not planned, but which meant more to us than any type of formal teaching. It stayed in my children's minds for weeks following, as each morning they would go to my kitchen window, scrape the frost from the glass, and look for the morning star.

I have thanked God often for that experience and for reminding me I am not to waste the opportunities which He gives me on a daily basis to share His Word with my children. All of God's creation proclaims His greatness. Yet so often we take for granted the object lessons which He places before us.

Cherish the Moment

Drawing on everyday circumstances to teach God's Word has been one of the most effective teaching methods I have used with my children. As we have witnessed God's power and majesty in operation, His love has become a living reality to our family.

Last summer our family vacationed in northwestern Ontario. One clear night, we all lay on the sandy beach beside a fire, looking up into a sky filled with millions of stars trying to outdo each other. We felt insignificant compared with the majesty of God displayed in His creation. We were filled with awe as we gazed at the Milky Way, something we rarely saw back home.

Psalm 19:1 came to mind: "The heavens are telling of the glory of God; and their expanse is declaring the work of His hands." And then, we shared Psalm 8:1, 3–6 with our children. We told them that they should always try to remember and cherish this moment, because God was telling us that no matter how unimportant or insignificant we might feel at different times, He has made us more beautiful than the stars in the heavens and He loves us.

O Lord, our Lord, how majestic is Thy name in all the earth, who hast displayed Thy splendor above the heavens! When I consider Thy heavens, the work of Thy fingers, the moon and the stars, which Thou hast ordained; what is man, that Thou dost take thought of him? And the son of man, that Thou dost care for him? Yet Thou hast made him a little lower than God, and dost crown him with glory and majesty! Thou dost make him to rule over the works of Thy hands; Thou hast put all things under his feet.

We all need this kind of personal touch with God through simple everyday experiences. We tend to forget that God is to be a part of our daily lives, and don't allow Him to teach us in the simple ways. Some people expect to learn of God only through intellectual means—Bible commentaries, Bible studies, sermons, etc. Although these methods are to be encouraged, we still need to have Jesus become part of our daily living.

For young children this is not difficult. They have all the time in the world and do not use this time to differentiate between what is spiritual and what is secular. To them it is all one. This is why it is so important that a mother should talk about God to her children as easily as she talks about food, clothing, or the weather. As she does this, the reality of God becomes easier for her child to grasp, and he naturally begins to apply the Scriptures to his surroundings.

Children need this encounter with God on a daily basis. They need to know that Jesus is not someone who lives only "in the sky," or in a church building, but that He lives with them, in their homes. Young children should begin to realize that Jesus is a special guest at their dinner table and hears every word they speak. He is at their side when they play, sleep, talk, and walk. He knows each of them by name and has the very hairs on their heads all counted. They need to know that His love is so great that He cares about such things as their fear of the dark or the loud noise the thunder makes, or the pain of skinned knees.

We need to tell them that all things were created to give praise to God. Even the brightly colored flowers and insignificant little bugs tell everyone about the creative power of God. In their innocent, uncluttered way, our children are able to understand the love God has for His creation which includes them.

A Joyful Mother

My own mother was an artist as she related to me the love of Jesus through my everyday surroundings. Each day's experience brought into my life a new teaching and understanding of God. The Holy Spirit used her to stir within my heart the childlike response to the message of God's love. Later that response grew into an adult commitment as the God of my childhood became the Lord and Saviour of my life.

Mother taught me the Parable of the Sower as we planted a garden (Luke 8:5–15). Later as we weeded that garden, she explained how weeds can be like sins that need to be pulled out. For the growth of weeds can choke out the young plant. I was that young plant and my life constantly needed weeding, she said. Often, Mother encouraged me to ask Jesus to pull the weeds of sin out of my life, as I confessed them to Him.

There were times of hurt in my life when someone would call me a bad name or push me down. Mother would comfort me, but would also use this as an opportunity to teach me about forgiving another person. As she held me in her arms and wiped away my tears, she would tell me what Jesus told us to do. "But I say to you who hear, love your enemies, do good to those who hate you, bless those who curse you, pray for those who mistreat you" (Luke 6:27). Although I didn't always like hearing those words, she was training me in one of the most important lessons I would ever learn about relationships with others.

One Easter, we received baby chickens from our grandmother. We put them in a little pen in our yard and diligently cared for them. One day as we were watching the chickens drink their water, Mom called our attention to the strange thing each chicken did after it took a drink. "Look," she said. "Are you watching what the chickens are doing?" We observed that each time they took a drink they would lift their little heads to the sky. They were unable to swallow the water unless they did this. My mother, who sensed that this was a time to teach her children another spiritual lesson explained: "God who made the chickens also created them to praise Him. When they raise their heads, doesn't it look like they are thanking God for the drink of water? When we have good things to eat and drink, we too say thank-you to God. That is why Daddy leads us in prayer before we eat." This explanation would probably not be acceptable to some theologians, but to an eight-year-old child, it made a lot of sense.

In these chapters, I am relating so much of what my mother taught me as a child. Actually this entire book is about her. She has never had the opportunity to write about any of her teaching techniques. To her it was just common sense. It was a way of life, a natural response to the love of God within her. She had an uncomplicated, natural approach to some very deep subjects.

This ability to use the naturalness of creation to teach the majesty and power of God was truly Holy Spirit inspired. Mother had a stirring within her which caused her to approach all of life from a spiritual point of view. Everything in life had meaning.

Flowers were not just flowers, or bugs just bugs. They were the handiwork of God and demanded our attention, respect, and our praise to their Maker.

Even things no one else seemed to consider beautiful, she talked about in special ways. She respected ants and snakes just as much as bumblebees and snowflakes. Everything had its purpose. Even dark clouds and thunderstorms were explained as majestic works of God.

Libby, the five-year-old daughter of a friend who was visiting us, was having a difficult time going to sleep. A thunderstorm was fast approaching and the wind and noise frightened her. Her mother had heard me explain to my own children the story my mother told me as a child about thunderstorms. In her desperation to quiet her fearful little girl, she came into my room and woke me. "Elise, could you please explain to Libby about the storms like you explained them to your children?" I took Libby into my arms and, as we lay on the bed facing the window, I began to relate to her what I so often told my frightened little ones, the story which my mother told to me over and over again.

My thoughts went back to my childhood and the many nights Mom would gather us into the living room during an approaching storm. Dad worked the midnight shift which intensified her fear of strong gusty winds and the possibility of a tornado. He was not available to calm the unrest she felt. To compensate for those fears, she used every creative ounce of strength she possessed to make the approaching storm a thing of beauty, so that we would learn to enjoy it rather than fear it.

All of us would go to a window in our large living room and watch the lightning flash across the sky and the wind begin to blow over the treetops. The clapping of the thunder was so loud it seemed as though the foundation of our house was shaking. As we were captivated by this display of God's power, Mom would begin her artistic description of the storm and its benefits to the earth. Sometimes the quivering in her voice made it difficult for her to start, but soon she spoke with confidence: "Isn't it wonderful the way God displays His power to the world? Why, even people who don't know God have to sit up and take notice. When thunder and lightning clash, God tells us He is still in charge. Isn't God powerful?"

She would then explain the benefits which a thunderstorm brings into our lives. A storm has beauty and character to it. Some are fierce and some are gentle. Some come quickly while others take a long time in building. She would tell us that a spring thunderstorm was God's special way of waking up all the little seeds which had just been planted in our garden. "It softens the ground and makes room for the roots of young plants to expand, so they find it easier to poke their little heads through the soil. These plants are thirsty and need a good drink of water." In my mind, I pictured each young plant holding its head high to receive a nice cool bath and drink. "They must be so thankful to God for the rain," I thought.

As much as my mother did not like lightning, she talked about its benefits to the earth and how it provided nitrogen for the soil, a necessary ingredient for all plants. In her opinion, everyone benefited from a storm, even the birds, who were delighted by puddles to take their baths in.

She made it appear that we had nothing to be afraid of, since God was in control. "Jesus has power over the wind and the rain," she reminded us. In a casual way, she would then tell us the incident of Jesus calming the wind and the waves when a violent storm erupted on the Sea of Galilee (Luke 8:22–26). "All Jesus had to say was, 'Peace, be still,' and the storm quieted. The disciples marveled that even the wind and the waves obeyed Him. He cared about His friends and used His power to help them."

Libby loved the story I told her. Since her grandfather was a farmer, she knew he would be thankful for the rain. The seeds he had planted in the spring needed a cool drink of water. Soon, she fell sound asleep, and once again I thanked God for my mother and the lessons she had taught me.

One time I related this incident to a young father. He replied, "Boy, your mom sure went through a lot of trouble to explain something very simple. All I ever tell my children about storms is that the thunder is a result of the 'angels bowling.'"

Because my mother explained God's creation to me in a joyful way, I grew to love the natural world. To this day, I find myself captivated with the power displayed in a building storm. My mother's patience, time, love, and simplistic explanations taught me to love things which could have been a source of great fear in my life.

Invest in Your Children

Using everyday situations to teach spiritual truths is a means of teaching which should never be underestimated. It is one of the most effective teaching tools available.

Jesus was a master in this art of teaching. He often spoke in parables, using everyday objects around Him to teach spiritual truths to His spiritual children, the disciples.

In confirmation class I learned that a parable is "an earthly story with a heavenly meaning." Jesus used earthly items such as vines and branches, sheep and shepherds, lost coins, mustard seeds, fig trees, brides, bridegrooms, and weddings to explain spiritual truths. He used stories, illustrations, and picture language to teach and prepare His spiritual children for a life of service to Him. Jesus wants us to be as children in our faith. Intellectualism is good only when it enhances a childlike response to God.

This particular method of teaching the Word of God to our children is not an easy one to use. It takes time. A mother may have to stop many times in a busy day to take advantage of particular circumstances. The dishes or dusting may have to wait, for teaching God's Word is of greater importance. You may see these interruptions as frustrations. However, in relationship to teaching spiritual truths, these interruptions are really investments in your child's spiritual life.

Another reason this type of teaching is difficult has to do with adult behavior. Most adults are very inhibited when it comes to sharing their faith with children in an informal setting. Most of us don't like to share our inner selves with anyone else. To express spiritual things in a childlike fashion feels particularly awkward.

Even though I grew up in a home where speaking of God's Word was an everyday experience, doing this with my own children is still difficult, at times. It has taken practice and a great deal of persistence to be able to express what I really feel inside about my relationship to the love of Jesus. Many times I have felt foolish and would have been embarrassed if I thought anyone but my children was listening to me. Adults just don't feel comfortable with this type of approach.

It is so important that you begin teaching your children early. Don't wait until they start Sunday School. Teaching them about Jesus begins when you first hold them in your arms. The earlier you begin and continue in this form of teaching your children, the easier it will be to teach them when they reach those self-conscious, noncommunicative teenage years.

When my little ones were just days old, I held them in my arms and I whispered to them that Jesus loved them. I sang them songs about Jesus. Even though I knew they could not comprehend with their minds what I was saying, I believed they could understand the love of God which I was expressing to them. I was beginning to prepare them for the day when they would recognize Jesus as their own personal Saviour.

By speaking frequently about the Lord to my infant children, I was also training myself to express my love for God in a verbal, childlike way, something I was not accustomed to doing.

In our home we have a large picture of Jesus. It was given to me by a favorite aunt as a graduation present from high school, and it has had an honored place in our house. Each one of our babies came to know this picture. From the time they were able to see, my husband and I would bring them to the picture and say, "Jesus loves you."

In our home little hands were taught how to be folded and little heads were taught to bow. Their first prayer was "Abba," an Aramaic word which Jesus used to address His Father. This two-syllable word became the beginning of their prayer life. As little as they were, they seemed to know the specialness of prayertime. Sometimes in our rush to go somewhere or do something, we would begin to eat without a blessing said. Our little ones would sit with their hands folded, waiting for us to begin our meal with prayer. Even juice and a cookie weren't eaten unless a prayer was said.

As soon as they started to talk we taught them the name of Jesus and encouraged them to express their love to Him in their own little ways, by saying His name softly and lovingly.

Music was an important part of those early years. They loved to sing with us and learned such songs as "Jesus Loves Me" and "This Little Gospel Light of Mine."

Interacting with my children on a spiritual level while they were very young paved the way for me to be able to share with them as teenagers. "Oatmeal and the Morning Star" probably would not have happened if these earlier interactions with them had not taken place.

5
Devotional Living

Christian families who desire family devotions to be a part of their daily lives find that the right time is seldom available. As a result, many of them give up trying, and then feel guilty.

A daily devotional time in which a family prays together and reads God's Word is a commendable goal for which to strive. But there is another way to teach God's Word which is also effective and meaningful. It was described by Moses as he gave the Israelites the commandments of God:

And you shall teach them diligently to your sons and shall talk of them when you sit in your house and when you walk by the way and when you lie down and when you rise up (Deuteronomy 6:7).

Deuteronomy 6 should be a great comfort for all of us who desire earnestly to share Jesus with our children and yet find conflicting schedules to be a real hindrance. It lays out a plan which I call Devotional Living, and is one way God has provided for us to live according to His Word on a day-by-day basis. From the time we rise in the early morning to when we go to sleep at night, we can teach our children the Word of God.

Devotional Living is the process of conveying spiritual truths throughout our daily experiences. The truths of God's Word are portrayed in the activities which take place in the home. Our senses become sharpened as we begin to recognize opportunities for talking about the message of salvation when we sit, walk, lie down, or rise up.

We all have the potential for this type of living, but we know too that it is not as easy as it sounds. Living is so daily. And there is a continual battle going on inside each of us—will we do our own thing or what God would have us do? What is so unique about being a Christian is that God gives us a choice. He doesn't impose His will on us, but wants us to freely choose His way and then receive the blessings He has promised. I hope that this book will help you to recognize God in the dailyness of your life, and to share your perceptions with your children.

Natural Expressions

What I remember most about the spiritual life in my parents' home, are the impromptu times when my mother shared her faith, and expressed her thankfulness for the blessings God bestowed upon her. She would weave together our daily experiences with words from the Bible. It was not a planned lesson, but a way of life for her. My early years were so saturated with experiences of this type that I found it natural to express myself in this same way.

Mother never stifled my response to God but was delighted when I felt free to love God in a childlike way without feeling ashamed or embarrassed. I mention this because mothers need to encourage their young children to express their love for Jesus in ways which might appear unnecessary or foolish to some adults.

When children are young, their minds and hearts are uninhibited and receptive to the things of God. They are so eager to absorb all of God's love, and willing to express it in charming and ingenuous ways.

It is this welling up inside that caused me, as a little child, to dance all the way from Sunday School. I would make up songs to Jesus about His flowers and birds. Sometimes I would twirl around, then stop to look at a bug crawling across the sidewalk. I had been made sensitive to God's creation and to His love for me, and God and I were having a great time. Those experiences hold a very special place in my memory even today.

As adults, we tend to hold back in expressing our love to God. We were created to praise Him and are told to become as "little children" in our faith. Could that mean that we are to become more like children in the way we express our love? It is so easy to stifle that childlike response because we feel certain behaviors are unacceptable in the adult world.

After Vacation Bible School had ended, a mother called to tell me about her five-year-old daughter. She had just learned the song, "I've Got the Joy, Joy, Joy, Joy Down in My Heart." After lunch, she went outside to play on her swing set. As she played, she sang this song as loudly as possible. This went on for quite some time before the mother thought she heard not just one voice but a chorus of little voices. Sure enough, there in her backyard was a group of children learning the song. The girl's response to what she had learned had drawn other children.

Early Beginnings
As children grow older, they lose this type of spontaneity. When they enter adolescence, they have to deal with changes which are taking place inside of them. We often stress the physical and emotional changes and tend to forget that there are also spiritual changes. During adolescence they are striving to be independent of us, and this is evidenced by their response when we make suggestions. Our once darling, expressive sons and daughters go into communication hibernation. Their verbal communication consists of grunts and sighs instead of distinguishable words. Charlie Shedd calls this noncommunicative period "the

caveman years." During this time it is especially difficult to get any expression from them in regard to their faith. Ask any Sunday School teacher of junior high students.

Our four children have gone through this phase. Instead of their response to spiritual matters being an emotional, verbal one, we saw an embarrassed look appear on their faces and an expression of "O Mom! Do I have to?"

This lack of verbal response worries many parents who want their children to react in the same way they did when they were younger. Expressions such as, "Read me another story about Jesus," or an enthusiastic, "Mommy, I love Jesus this much!" are no longer there.

During this phase, young teenagers are doing a lot of thinking. They are in the process of growing up, making decisions for themselves, wanting to express themselves in ways which are uniquely their own. The Holy Spirit is at work in their hearts preparing them for a personal response to the love of Jesus which was instilled when they were small children.

You can prepare for these difficult teenage years by establishing devotional living within the home when your children are small. The sooner you start this process the more background you will give them. You are laying a foundation on which they can build their lives.

If you wait until your children are older to share Jesus with them, the task will be much more difficult. I am not saying that it will be impossible, but it will require more time, take a great deal more perseverance, and surely not be as much fun.

Make up your mind to begin now. You will not only be giving them a necessary foundation for their life in Christ, but you will be learning along with them how to express your faith. Believe me, it is much easier to express your faith to a small child for the first time than to a teenager.

Also, your children will become accustomed to hearing you speak about spiritual things, and will learn to regard this as normal behavior from you.

It's an exciting adventure on which you are embarking. The Holy Spirit will produce in you a creativity which you didn't know you possessed. He will make you sensitive and give you a keen awareness of the many possibilities available.

Seeing the Obstacles

It may prove helpful if you understand some of the very common obstacles which many of us have to overcome before we feel comfortable with devotional living.

• The first obstacle is a feeling of embarrassment when expressing ourselves in a spiritual way. Many of us need to have our tongues trained. Spiritual phrases such as, "Thank You, Jesus, for the sunshine, snowflakes, flowers," or "Jesus loves you," "God bless you," "God be with you," are too often absent from our vocabulary. We need practice in speaking them, so that they become a comfortable part of life.

At first I found this difficult to do, but after much repetition it became easier. I began by praying with each one of my babies, and telling them how much Jesus loved them. At night I would place my hand on their little heads and whisper, "God be with you." As they grew older, their response was always positive and this encouraged me. They loved to hear me talk about Jesus, for the presence of His love was something they enjoyed. As they cuddled close to me, my feelings of self-consciousness melted away.

Their age was definitely a plus for me. They were too young to criticize. Soon the little expressions I used became a natural part of my speaking, and I no longer felt self-conscious. Now that they are teenagers, they hear a "God bless you" or "God be with you" on a daily basis, as they leave for school or go on a date.

• Another obstacle which we have to deal with is our impatience. We want everything to take place at once. If you are starting from scratch, take time to draw close to Jesus through your praying and reading of the Word. You will soon experience the "rivers of living water" welling up inside. It won't be long before you will want this to become verbal in your daily experiences with your children.

• You may find that one of the hindrances to sharing your faith with your children is your inability to see things through their eyes. As adults we are very inhibited and feel uncomfortable in expressing the things of God in an emotional way. Many of the analogies or illustrations I use with my children may seem silly to many adults. A pseudosophistication may prevent us from using language and imagery which children can understand.

Sitting in the middle of a kitchen floor with little ones on your lap singing "Praise Him" may seem a bit weird to some people. But children are enthralled by praising God for flowers and tiny bugs and thunderstorms, and doing so builds memories for them.

There are three things to remember as you begin.

• Spend time getting to know Jesus better.

• Realize that spiritual communication with your children will not just happen. It takes practice.

• Start when your children are very little.

Many of the ideas in this book have worked with my children. Beyond their teaching value, they have been a joy and have created precious memories for all of us. This concept of devotional living was sometimes a spark of light in a dark place of despair. Jesus was with us wherever we went. He was present in our home when it was filled with crying, unhappy children; while we planted our garden; as we drove in a car—which sometimes died in the middle of an intersection; and in the quiet times of loving and meeting each other's needs.

Not all of my suggestions will meet the needs of your family, for you are unique. As God works with you as an individual, He will meet the specific needs which your family has. Please consider my ideas simply as a jumping-off point for you to begin to discover meaningful ways to present Jesus to your children.

Appreciating Beauty

In his book *Celebration of Discipline,* Richard J. Foster comments that Christians too often fail to recognize the beauty of the natural world which God has provided. We take so much for granted, seldom stopping to appreciate the beauty around us. In our technological society, some of us are more aware of the wonders of a computer than of the complexity of God's creation.

Foster points out that "God who made the heavens and earth uses His creation to show us something of His glory and give us something of His life" (Harper and Row, p. 25). Nature is one of the simplest and most ancient ways that God speaks. The trouble is that most people are not quiet long enough to listen.

Many of David's psalms speak of creation praising God. Psalm 148 declares that the heavens, the angels, sun, moon, and stars praise God. The earth echoes its praises as well. The sea monsters, fire, hail, snow, clouds, stormy winds, mountains and hills, fruit trees, the beasts and all cattle, creeping things and winged animals, kings of earth, young men, virgins, old men and children—"Let them praise the name of the Lord, for His name alone is exalted; His glory is above earth and heaven" (v. 13).

City dwellers have a hard time seeing God in their surroundings—dirty snow, garbage trucks, fenced-in yards, cement streets and sidewalks, crowded shopping malls and multilevel expressways. A sunset is usually obstructed from view by high-rise buildings, and stargazing is almost impossible through the pollution.

I often long for the beauty which surrounded our family in New Guinea. We were reminded of God as we witnessed waterfalls springing from the face of the mountains. Sunrises and sunsets were awesome. The night sky during the dry season was a display case for the billions of stars. Wild flowers grew in abundance and rushing streams sang their songs of praise as they moved through the mountainside.

Far from the industrial world we lived with God's power and majesty portrayed in our surroundings. Everywhere we turned nature was shouting out the praises of its Creator. We saw the power of God as the ground around us shook and swayed during an earth tremor, and we were reminded of His goodness when it finally stopped and we could breathe a little easier.

City people can plan experiences to help their children become sensitive to God's love for them through creation. Several mothers who didn't have transportation available during the day planned an outing in a nearby park. One mother didn't feel the park offered the quietness and beauty which she desired, but not far from her home was a cemetery. Now and then she would pack a picnic lunch and take her children there for a walk. With peanut butter sandwiches in their hands, they would marvel at the birds, flowers, and the quiet beauty.

To some people this may seem a strange place to go. The reminder of death frightens them. After all, ghost stories usually take place in cemeteries. Certainly, we don't want to scare our children. But along with the teaching which we give them about nature, in such a place can come the beautiful teaching of the resurrection from the dead which Christ has promised to us who believe.

A walk or drive through a wooded area on a brisk fall day to admire the changing color can provide an awareness of God's creative hand in nature. We often explained to our young children that the turning of the leaves was God's way of painting a beautiful picture for us.

You can also tell your children how God wondrously cares for His creation.

He counts the number of the stars;
He gives names to all of them.
Great is our Lord, and abundant in strength. . . .
Who covers the heavens with clouds,
Who provides rain for the earth,
Who makes grass to grow on the mountains.
He gives to the beast its food,
And to the young ravens which cry (Psalm 147:4–5, 8–9).

God loves and cares for the animals. Not one sparrow ever falls from the sky without His knowing about it. He loves puppies, squirrels, and even tiny ants. They all have food provided for them and places of shelter.

I was taught as a child never to mistreat any animal or to cruelly allow one to suffer. Sometimes a hornet or bee would enter our home during the summer. My mother would often take the time to catch it in a towel and shake it out the window so that it could be free. It would have been so easy for her to kill it. Afterward, she would explain how God created the bees and wasps to pollinate the flowers and plants.

My children have often watched the ants work and have observed how painstakingly they carry their food to their underground homes. I told the children that God created us to work as diligently as these ants. Work is a gift from Him. Proverbs 6:6 says:

Go to the ant, O sluggard,
Observe her ways and be wise,
Which, having no chief,
Officer or ruler,
Prepares her food in the summer,
And gathers her provision in the harvest.

One morning, after a torrential rain had hit our area, we had many large puddles. Johnny was watching the activity in our backyard, until all filled to the brim with excitement, he called out: "Mommy, the birdies are taking a bath in our yard. Quick, come and see!" The sparrows were having a delightful time, flapping their wings and splashing the warm water over their feathers.

In another part of the yard, something else was taking place that Johnny called a "birdie picnic," as the robins pulled worms from the earth.

As the other children gathered to watch, I told them to listen carefully to the sound of the birds singing and chirping. The air seemed filled with a chorus of thankful praise. It was a pleasant experience for our family that quiet morning, one which caused Matthew 6:25–26 to come alive in our hearts.

For this reason I say to you, do not be anxious for your life, as to what you shall eat, or what you shall drink; nor for your body, as to what you shall put on. Is not life more than food, and the body than clothing? Look at the birds of the air, that they do not sow, neither do they reap, nor gather into barns, and yet your heavenly Father feeds them. Are you not worth much more than they?

My friend Joyce appreciates nature more than anyone else I know. Quite often she will call and tell me to stop what I'm doing just to see the sun setting. Or as we drive along, usually in a hurry to get somewhere, she will pull her car off the road to watch a deer in the forest, or a display of wild flowers along the road. She has trained her senses to be aware of nature and the aesthetic beauty it holds. She has also taught her children to be sensitive to lovely things. One day when we had stopped along the road, her daughter explained to me, "Mom told us that whenever we see something beautiful we are supposed to stop and take a long look at it so that we will always remember."

Fireflies fascinate my children. Many years ago while driving through a long stretch of farmland on a hot summer night, we saw entire fields lit up with their tiny blinking lights. Of course, we talked about what makes the fireflies light up. The next day we went to the library to find some answers.

A rainbow is something which should be explained to children. Every time a rainbow appears, it is a reminder to us of God's grace and promise. And it is a good time to tell the story of Noah and the first rainbow, from Genesis 9:13–16.

Snowflakes have always fascinated me. The descending flakes falling on our eyelids and faces sensitize us to the softness of God's creation. He could very well dump all the snow at one time, but instead, He chooses to allow one flake at a time to make its soft descent to the ground. After examining the many different shapes and forms I am amazed that God makes each one different. "Just like us," I would say. "He has made us all unique."

In the city, snow gets dirty in a hurry. When a new snow falls, everything looks white again. I have explained to my children how our sin makes us dirty before our holy God, but the blood of Jesus is like a brand new snowfall. Jesus takes away the "dirtiness" of sin in our lives, making us pure white before Him. As Isaiah 1:18 says: "Though your sins are as scarlet, they will be as white as snow."

I have told my children that everything—mountains, valleys, the wind, a babbling brook, lightning, thunder—was designed to praise God. The mountains raise their faces high and the valleys bow down low before God. The trees clap their hands and raise their arms to God. The rivers and brooks offer a song of praise. All we have to do is take the time to recognize it.

Praise Walks

Praise Walks were a common experience for my children. As we walked, we watched for things for which to praise God.

Paul would see a ladybug on his sleeve. "Thank You, Jesus, for the ladybug," he would say. Elisabeth would notice a butterfly. "Look, Mommy. He's so pretty. May I catch him?" To which I would reply: "You'll hurt him if you touch his pretty wings. Let him fly freely the way God created him to fly. We can just watch and enjoy him." "Thank You, Jesus, for the butterfly," would be Elisabeth's response.

Sometimes they gave praise for funny shaped stones and rocks. These were real treasures for David who loved to put them in his pockets and carry them home.

Often we would lie on our backs and observe the clouds. Each one had a different shape. When my children wondered if clouds were soft like cotton balls, I was able to tell them what clouds were made of. Watching the clouds was also a time to explain the ascension of Jesus. He ascended into the clouds and was hid from the disciples as He was taken up into heaven (Acts 1:9). But the promise was given by two angels that Jesus would return in the same way He had been taken up (1:11). When we look at the clouds we should be reminded of His glorious Second Coming.

Gardening

Working together in a garden is a time for learning spiritual lessons. In Matthew 13, Jesus described a farmer sowing seed in a field. The seed represents the Word of God and the soil depicts the hearts of men. As we would turn over the soil in our garden, breaking up the large clumps of dirt, I would explain how our hearts need to be soft, loose, fertile soil, so that when the Word of God is planted, it will be able to take root and grow.

As we planted the seeds, we talked about the ways God's Word comes into our hearts—through Sunday School lessons, in church on Sunday, when Mom and Dad speak about Jesus. We all should listen and ask the Holy Spirit to make our hearts fertile ground.

We would ask God to bless our little garden and to cause it to grow. And we would talk about the miracle of growth which takes place as a result of the warm sunshine, air, rain, and fertilizer. The little seeds and seedlings look so insignificant; yet, in a matter of weeks, they will be on their way to becoming full-grown plants with the ability to reproduce themselves many times over.

God's multiplication is the same in our lives as Christians. When we plant seeds of love, faith, and generosity, God blesses us abundantly. Second Corinthians 9:10–11 describes this multiplication process:

Now He who supplies seed to the sower and bread for food, will supply and multiply your seed for sowing and increase the harvest of your righteousness; you will be enriched in everything for all liberality, which through us is producing thanksgiving to God.

Seeds also must die before they are able to begin the growth process. Jesus said,

Unless a grain of wheat falls into the earth and dies, it remains by itself alone; but if it dies, it bears much fruit. He who loves his life loses it; and he who hates his life in this world shall keep it to life eternal (John 12:24–25).

Our life is like that seed. We must die daily to sin and be raised up with Jesus to a new life (Romans 6:4; Colossians 2:12).

Hoeing and weeding the garden are not children's favorite activities. They would rather plant and see the results of growing seedlings. But it is such an easy thing to allow a garden to become overgrown by weeds. The little plants are then starved for light, and have no room to send down their tiny roots. So it is with sin in our lives. Sometimes we would rather not bother with removing it. But if we are lazy Christians and allow it to grow in our hearts, the Word of God is choked out. Just as the weeds must be removed from our garden, sin needs to be confessed and removed from our lives so that the Word of God will be able to grow in us.

Many times my children would have a hard time distinguishing the plants from weeds that somehow disguised themselves among the growing plants. I would tell them, "Sin is like that in our lives. We sometimes think a wrong action is good. We don't want to give up a certain sin. But when the Holy Spirit causes us to recognize it as wrong, that particular 'weed' or sin must be pulled out no matter how much we like it. We must not allow it to grow."

Harvesting the crop is one of the best times in gardening, when the blessing of our labor becomes evident. Everything matures nicely and we thank God for taking care of our little garden. It also provides us with the opportunity to share our abundance with others.

In Scripture, the harvest relates to Christ's Second Coming (Mark 4:26–29). When the "harvest" is ready, Christ will return.

It also refers to people who would believe if someone would tell them. Matthew 9:37–38 states that "the harvest is plentiful, but the workers are few. Therefore, beseech the Lord of the harvest to send out workers into His harvest."

The fields are "white for harvest" (John 4:35). When wheat is ready to be harvested, it takes on a white glow. There are people who are like that ripened wheat, who are ready to hear the Word. God wants us to be ready to go and to proclaim the message of salvation, to be His harvesters, to be soul-winners for Him.

Nature offers some of the best opportunities for sharing your faith with your children. You will discover many more ways than have been explored in this chapter. Pray for a sensitivity to the things around you and God will open your eyes. You are not only teaching them to praise God, but to understand about sin and forgiveness, and about scriptural motivations to service.

6
You Are My Brother and I Love You

It doesn't take any mother long to recognize that her children have been born with sinful natures which need to be dealt with on a regular basis. This becomes especially evident when two children are playing together. If they both want the same toy, a real tug-of-war can take place, complete with kicking, screaming, hair pulling, and even biting. Usually the stronger child wins, leaving the weaker one in tears and frustration.

The battle which has taken place is more than a struggle over a toy. It is a contest for rights, which will continue into adult life. If not dealt with, a child who continually exerts his rights over another is headed for trouble.

Mothers sometimes regard their little angels as perfect. How could they be capable of doing anything wrong? In my experience with four children, I have found that I never had to instruct any of them in the fine art of sinning. It came quite naturally.

The Bible clearly states, "All have sinned and fall short of the glory of God" (Romans 3:23), and "There is none righteous, not even one" (3:10). The Bible does not put any age limit on sinning. The word *all* indicates everyone is guilty. Sin is a part of the natural self, the old man, our human natures. That small children do not consciously understand sin does not exempt them from it. Their little wills, which are so defiant and rebellious toward authority, have to be brought under subjection.

This is one of the most laborious aspects of childrearing and one of the most crucial. A child who has not learned obedience and submission to authority will have a rough time living as a Christian when he matures.

We are not doing our children any favors by ignoring sin in their lives. Children who are not disciplined will suffer. (See Proverbs 13:18, 24; 19:18, 27; 22:15; 23:13–14; 29:17.) Not only will the children suffer, but the mother who does not discipline her children will be brought to shame. "The rod and reproof give wisdom, but a child who gets his own way brings shame to his mother" (Proverbs 29:15).

Jesus had to learn obedience. Born with a human nature, He was God and man at the same time. As a result of His human nature, He was tempted to sin. He had the potential for committing sin, but because He was God, He resisted sin and led the perfect life for us, and took our sins upon Himself at the cross.

Jesus lived in obedience to His heavenly Father and to earthly parents. He suffered much for our sake. Obedience was not always easy. The Bible says, "Although He was a Son, He learned obedience from the things which He suffered" (Hebrews 5:8). This type of obedience made Him submissive to the will of His Father. Eventually it cost His life on the cross for the sins of the world.

Our children should be in the process of learning obedience from the things which they will have to suffer. They will resist our teaching. No child or adult likes to be corrected or made to do certain things. It is against nature. Through discipline, children learn to resist certain things they desire, and move toward what God wills for them.

God does not put any age limit when sin should begin to be

dealt with. The commandments which apply to adults also apply to children. It is necessary that children learn what is acceptable and unacceptable behavior in the eyes of God. They need to be trained in righteousness and to see the consequences of sin in their lives.

If sin is not dealt with on a regular basis, a child's sinful nature is then allowed to develop and grow. Rebellion, self-centeredness, self-indulgence, lack of self-control, and other negative behaviors will eventually become an established way of life, resistant to change.

As mothers, part of our job is to train our children to react against the desires of their flesh, so that the qualities of the Christian life have room to grow.

My goal in disciplining our children has been to teach them self-control, so that they may be able to live in conformity to the Word of God. Discipline produces godly character (1 Timothy 4:7-8). I want the qualities of Christ to be a part of my children's lives.

Discipline is a type of devotional living within the framework of the family experience. Through discipline, children learn many lessons which will later be applied to their adult lives. As we use the Scriptures to teach them what sin is, its consequences, and the forgiving love of God in Christ Jesus, they are learning how to resist temptation and say no to sin.

Through discipline they learn that it is not right to hit someone or to call another person a name, even to defend their rights. They learn to put other people first and to love and bless those who dislike them.

Our homes are to be the training grounds for this type of behavior. As we teach our children through repetition and practice, we are training their senses to discern good from evil (Hebrews 5:14).

Parents who allow name-calling, teasing, arguing, and physical abuse to be a normal part of their children's behavior are in reality training them in ways which are not pleasing to Christ. I realize that all children participate in such actions. My own children are excellent examples of this. But Christian parents should not openly permit a child to indulge in sin.

The home should never be a place where children are given the license to sin. The world will give them enough reinforcement in sinning. The home needs to stand against sin. The rules for the godly life should be practiced within the confines of the home, using God's Word as the basis for behavior.

This process of training or disciplining children is a difficult one, requiring a great deal of time and perseverance. The easy way out is to ignore behavior problems. Some parents are lazy and excuse their children's bad behavior by saying that it is just a stage they will eventually grow out of. What they don't realize is that one stage usually grows into another until the stages become the problem. Behavior problems naturally fester and grow, if left alone. Parents who let nature take its course may later reap the whirlwind, in problems that no one can solve.

In our four children, I saw what the sinful nature of a child is all about. Sibling rivalry, usually stemming from jealousy, and a desire to please oneself, were the prominent characteristics displayed each day. They fought over toys, and their games usually ended in cruel words—they generally were poor losers and complained about the winner. Teasing, name-calling, and fighting were frequent. Each child, it seemed, thought only of himself and what was best for him.

I was often exhausted at the end of a day just from refereeing their squabbles. Sometimes a sense of guilt would sweep over me as I lay in bed at night recalling the events of a day and wondering if I was a mean mother. Their little wills had to be brought under authority. I was convinced that they should not get away with behavior which was contrary to God's Word, even if it was "a natural part of their growing up." To allow them to act upon impulse and "do their own thing" would actually be doing them a disservice. I loved them too much to allow that to happen.

When I now watch our four teenagers, I thank God for making me persistent in disciplining them. I refused to allow them the freedom to do as they pleased. They have been taught to live by God's rules, not mine or the world's. They have been trained, by practice and repetition, to discern good from evil, as we have used the Word of God as the basis for right and wrong.

I have seen a sensitivity develop in their lives which has carried over to people outside the family. They have learned to respect human life, realizing that fighting back is not always the answer to getting their own way. Despite the difficulty of putting into practice what they know in their hearts to be true, they have seen God bless them as they have submitted to His will.

Their sinful natures have not disappeared. They will always be there until the children enter eternity with Jesus. But the little problems of 10 and 15 years ago have not matured into big problems. I'm sure you have heard the saying, "Little kids— little problems, big kids—big problems." Most people believe that. However, if the little problems are nipped in the bud, they will not grow into big ones.

Loving Discipline

One thing we must remember about discipline is that no child will receive it with joy. I do not welcome discipline in my own life even though I know it is good for me. It hurts when the Holy Spirit reveals sin to me through the Word or through another person. I do not like to change, and have gone through some pretty rough times in the past because of my unwillingness to submit to God's will for my life.

God disciplines me because He loves me (Hebrews 12:6). He does not want me to be spiritually immature, unable to discern right from wrong. He has a plan for my life; but to follow it, I need to be trained to obey Him.

As parents, we are to follow God's pattern for discipline in correcting our children. We discipline them because we love them and want to see perfected in them the "peaceful fruit of righteousness" (Hebrews 12:11). When we neglect this aspect of caring for our children, we are really being disobedient to God's will and are honoring our children above the Lord.

In the Old Testament book of 1 Samuel, the story is told about a priest named Eli who did not rebuke his sons. Eli, it was said, honored his sons above the Lord (2:29). Instead of disciplining and training them, he allowed them to do whatever they pleased, and they grew up to be "worthless men" (2:12). As a result, God cut off the household of Eli from the priesthood. What grieving must have taken place within the soul of Eli (2:33). Many mothers today grieve within their souls because of children who grew up without discipline.

Children need to know the rules and boundaries. They will use every opportunity to test you, but will also have a great respect for your consistency if you refuse to be swayed by pouting and tears.

A story was told to me by a mother who knew the importance of not wavering from a decision, especially when you are sure it is right. Her eight-year-old daughter came bouncing into the kitchen one day requesting to do something with her friends which she knew her mother would never allow. To the reply of no, the little girl began to cry and accuse her mother of not being fair. After all, her friends' mothers thought it was OK. Her mother was the only mean one.

When she saw her mother standing her ground, she thought of another tactic. Stomping off to her room and slamming the door would certainly convince her mother to give in.

A few minutes passed by and another attempt was made. "Please, Mother, can I do it?" "No," was her mother's reply.

The little girl, knowing that she had lost this battle, left the kitchen in a huff. Her mother, convinced that she had done the right thing, listened curiously to her daughter's explanation to her friends waiting in the backyard. To her amazement, her daughter proudly announced, "See, I told you my mother wouldn't let me go."

There are so many ways in which discipline can be administered to children. Each family is different and each child is unique. But there are some things about discipline which should remain constant, whatever the present situation.

• The particular transgression the child has committed needs to be pointed out and explained as sin.

• Proper disciplinary action needs to take place in order to teach the child that his behavior was not right. This disciplinary action should be administered in love, not in anger. The child needs to know that you love him throughout the disciplining procedure.

• Forgiveness needs to be announced, forgiveness from Jesus and from the parents.

• Some form of physical love should be expressed to the child after forgiveness is announced. This physical contact assures your child of your love.

Begin young in your children's lives to discipline them. Take advantage of those early years. If you wait until they are old enough to understand the concept of sin, you are many years too late.

You Are My Brother and I Love You

Learning to love those who are the closest to us can present some real friction, especially among brothers and sisters. If there was any place I wanted my children to learn how to love others it was in our home. They needed to be taught how to love and respect one another and to express this to each other.

I have always figured that if my children could take time to hurt each other, they could also learn to take time to express their love. Children by instinct retaliate when an injustice is done to them. They think of no other recourse than to strike back. They need to be taught to do exactly the opposite of what their human nature is urging them to do.

Constant contact with brothers and sisters usually results in feeling bored with one another, and that's when squabbles, cross words, and fighting surface. Many times as my children would quarrel, I would allow them to try to settle their differences without my interference. I felt this was a learning experience. But whenever they began to hurt one another either through their words or actions, I would intervene.

I never asked who was right or wrong, but approached the conflict from the standpoint of how Jesus would want us to act. "He wants us to love each other, not to hurt one another. Even if another person hits you, you are not given the right to hit him back. Jesus was whipped and called bad names, but He didn't hurt anyone back. He loved us so much that He willingly died for us. We are to act just like Jesus did," I said. "We are to love each other as Jesus loves us."

After hearing both sides of the story I explained that regardless of who was right or wrong in the beginning, everyone was really wrong because of the hateful way they had reacted. Name-calling and hitting are not part of our life in Jesus. We are to love others even when they don't love us back.

You may think that young children will not be able to understand this principle. After all, this is difficult for any adult to put into practice, much less a child.

Just remember—they don't have to understand everything at the beginning. You don't require that they understand why you put them to bed each night at 7:30. You just do it and they accept it. As they mature in their understanding, they begin to comprehend. Just because your children disagree with something doesn't mean that you stop doing it. Their little natures must be trained in the spiritual as well as in the physical.

After you explain that what they did was wrong and how this

has been sin before God, you need to tell them that Jesus came to take that sin. Jesus forgives them when they ask for forgiveness.

It is important that they forgive one another and physically express their love to each other. This little exercise was required of my children each time they verbally or physically hurt someone in the family.

The two people involved in the squabble were required to hold hands and look each other square in the eye. This was so difficult for them to do, but eye contact is extremely important. They were each required to say: "You are my brother and I love you. I'm sorry I hit you and I will try not to do it again." They were not allowed to leave until this process was totally completed by both offenders.

Sometimes they got very stubborn. They garbled their words, and looked down at their feet. But before they could be dismissed, each person had to speak it clearly, and the situation be resolved.

Usually after several attempts at saying the sentence, the giggling began, and everyone relaxed. Finally, each child had to physically love the other by giving a big hug. What a difference had taken place in a few minutes. They began in tears and anger and left with giggles and smiles.

One of our big surprises came when Warren and I had a nonverbal argument going—the kind which conveys messages through body language. It was obvious to our children what was taking place, and they didn't like it. Their solution for getting us on loving terms again was the same technique I had used with them for years. In the middle of our kitchen they made us hold hands and look each other square in the eye. I had to say, "You are my husband and I love you. I'm sorry and I will try not to do it again." Warren repeated the same thing to me, and then we hugged each other. I still remember the tears that welled up in my eyes as God healed our relationship through this simple act. It had worked for so many years in the lives of our children and now we were benefiting from it.

Love and Bless Your Enemies

It is easy enough to ask God to bless your enemies when they live in faraway countries. It is another thing to ask God to bless someone you deal with on a daily basis, who isn't nice to you. Sometimes that person is a neighbor, relative, teacher, playmate, or family member. Not everyone in the world is going to like you, and there may even be someone who is out to persecute you.

Children are not exempt from hurt of this type. Over and over again they may have to deal with people who are unkind to them.

Jesus teaches us and our children how to deal with the "people problem,"

But I say to you who hear, love your enemies, do good to those who hate you, bless those who curse you, pray for those who mistreat you. . . . If you love those who love you, what credit is that to you? For even sinners love those who love them. And if you do good to those who do good to you, what credit is that to you? For even sinners do the same thing. But love your enemies, and do good, and lend, expecting nothing in return; and your reward will be great (Luke 6:27, 32–33, 35).

Those are pretty tough words to live by, and many times I have asked God if He really expects me to do all that. My human nature rebels.

You may feel that this lesson is too difficult to teach your child. The general thinking is that a child needs to learn to fight back or else he will grow up being walked all over.

Does a child really need to be taught to fight back? I don't think he does. Even the most timid child will eventually strike back in defense when pushed far enough. It is naturally in him to retaliate. A child needs to be taught the opposite. God says not to strike back. We are to ask Him to bless those who harm us.

David was always my easiest child to deal with. His temperament was such that he was sensitive to others and wanted to please. He was definitely not the fighting type. Upon our return from New Guinea, he encountered a difficult situation at school. A particular child teased him unmercifully, and David responded with a few punches.

I talked to David and encouraged him to walk away from the boy the next time the teasing began. "This is what God would want you to do," I explained. I felt cruel telling him to do that, but I also knew that David had to learn the same lessons which I had to learn. I told him that Jesus commanded us in His Word to love our enemies, to bless them, and even turn the other cheek when someone else hits us. He gave me a quizzical look, wondering if I really understood.

We prayed and asked God to bless Tony and to help David with his problem. This was not easy for me and took every ounce of my strength to say it. But I trusted God that He would bless my obedience.

Each night we asked God to bless Tony. Still the teasing persisted and David continued to sometimes fight back and sometimes walk away. But, thanks be to God, results began to appear. The problem was resolved in a fairly short time and Tony and David actually became friends.

It is not easy for children to pray for someone who is mistreating them. They don't understand it; but then again, they don't have to understand it. It is something which God requires of them. When we submit to God's way, He has the responsibility of working it out.

Our children need to be taught this principle with patience and gentleness. It is training for them. If they learn this concept early, it becomes easier for them to handle difficult relationships in their adult lives.

Dwell on the Fine and the Good

Unkind words so easily slip out of our mouths. A lot of verbal abuse takes place in some homes between brothers and sisters. Often teasing is so intense that an outburst of anger erupts. Just because this is a common experience, a natural part of growing up, does not mean it should be tolerated. "Let no unwholesome word proceed from your mouth, but only such a word as is good for edification according to the need of the moment, that it may give grace to those who hear" (Ephesians 4:29).

Words such as "Dummy," "Stupid," "Ugly," "Retard," or any forms of foul language so prevalent today should not be allowed in your home. It is so easy to find fault with one's peers. Our children are just as guilty as any others. I am continually dealing with the abuse of words in our family.

The way we have learned to handle this particular problem in our home is by counteracting every bad word with a good one. We base this on Philippians 4:8:

Finally, brethren, whatever is true, whatever is honorable, whatever is right, whatever is pure, whatever is lovely, whatever is of good repute, if there is any excellence and if anything worthy of praise, let your mind dwell on these things.

When a derogatory word is said about another person, I make the person who said it counteract it by saying something especially nice about that one. Often he will whisper in a muffled tone, and so I make him say it again and again until it is audible.

John must have been about six years old when he called Elisabeth a bad name at the dinner table. He realized what he had done. We heard it, Elisabeth heard it, and so did Paul and David. He knew we were displeased and without our having to say one word to him, he softly whispered to Elisabeth, "And you have pretty blonde hair."

Warren and I chuckled. At that young age, John had already been trained that he could not get away with this type of behavior. Without our telling him to do so, he corrected himself.

Forgiving One Another

One hot summer afternoon after refereeing several squabbles, I really became disgusted with the behavior of my children. They were being anything but kind to one another. Every time they began to play a game, someone got angry.

Finally, I sat them down around my kitchen table and explained to them that their behavior was extremely displeasing to me and to God. He didn't want us to act in such a way. I wanted them to find out for themselves how God wanted them to act. I gave each one who could read a New Testament and had them read out loud together Ephesians 4:32.

There in front of them were the words: "And be kind to one another, tender-hearted, forgiving each other, just as God in Christ also has forgiven you."

They all knew what it meant, even though the idea was difficult for them to verbalize. I had them silently read verse 31 about putting away all the bitterness and wrath and anger. They knew they were wrong, and that they needed to be reconciled. They had sinned by treating each other in an unkind manner.

"Now, I want you all to say a silent prayer asking God to forgive you and to give you the power not to do it again." After a few moments of silence came the responses, "I'm sorry. Can I go now?"

The process had to be repeated that day, but I was not going to give in to disobedience. They were being trained and I knew God was going to bless my persistence.

You won't always think you are succeeding. In fact, you may think nothing has been accomplished. Don't judge success by the response you get. It's not the response which counts but your obedience to the commands of God to discipline your children. You are training them now, when they are young, to be obedient Christians.

God has blessed our family with lots of physical expressions of love between family members. The training process has been tedious, difficult, and long, but it has paid off. Our children have learned to stand against the wants of their human natures. God is working and I trust that the work He has begun will be brought to full bloom and maturity in their adult lives.

7
I Feel Like
an Only Child

Eight grown brothers and sisters came to mourn the passing of their aged mother whom they dearly loved. As they were together after the funeral, their sadness seemed to melt away as they told the happy memories of their childhood, and reminisced about the love which was radiated to them from their mother.

After several had related fond memories, one of the sons announced, "I don't know how Mom did it. She had so many of us to care for, and yet she always made me feel like an only child."

"You mean you felt that way too?" asked one of his sisters. "I thought I was the only one." They were all amazed to find that their mother had had the unique ability to make each child feel like an only child!

To impress upon a child that he is unique, wanted, loved, and special helps him to grow into an adult who loves himself as God intended. In learning to love himself, he in turn is able to reach out with this love to others.

This good self-concept which has been implanted helps him

understand the love of God. As a result of the love which has been expressed to him primarily through his mother, he is able to understand how very special he is to God.

Making children feel special does not excuse the sin in their lives. What it does is to make them aware of the grace of God. They learn that God's love for them is present even when they do wrong. God's grace—God's *R*iches *A*t *C*hrist's *E*xpense—is not available to them as a result of their goodness, but because of God's goodness and love. While we were still in our sin, Christ died for us (Ephesians 2:5; Romans 5:8). The sin still needs to be pointed out, but in the context of forgiveness and grace which are greater than our sin.

Touching Your Children

A child begins to recognize his specialness very early in life. At birth, as the mother holds, cuddles, kisses, and talks to her baby, she is conveying to him how very dear he is.

Selma Fraiberg in her book *Every Child's Birthright: In Defense of Mothering,* says this about the importance of loving and touching our babies early in life:

During the first six months, the baby has the rudiments of a love language available to him. There is the language of the embrace, the language of the eyes, the language of the smile, vocal communications of pleasure and distress. It is the essential vocabulary of love before we can speak of love. Eighteen years later, when this baby is full grown and "falls in love" for the first time, he will woo his partner through the language of the eyes, the language of the smile, through the utterance of endearments, and the joy of the embrace.

In his declarations of love he will use such phrases as: "When I first looked into your eyes," "When you smiled at me," "When I held you in my arms." And naturally, in his exalted state, he will believe that he invented this love song (Bantam, p. 29).

Touching, especially in the beginning years of life, is one of the best things which we can do for our children. Their skin cries out for it. Babies have been known to die from lack of touch. Others who have experienced long periods without some type of personal contact show abnormal behavior patterns. Some become withdrawn and sullen; others become rockers, banging their heads against walls and furniture.

Young people whose skin-hunger needs are satisfied tend to be open, warm and relaxed. Those who have been rarely touched at home often seem to be more withdrawn, prone to living in a fantasy world, even hostile. I am convinced that they have a diminished sense of their own worth. You can see them on any playground—kids who seem absolutely devoted to tripping each other, shoving, wrestling, and fighting. Inside the schools they push each other down the stairs, shove faces into the drinking fountains, throw food in the lunchroom. And behind every shove and trip there is an unheard cry of skin hunger (Sidney B. Simon, *Caring, Feeling, Touching*, Argus Communications).

During World War I, there was an orphanage in Europe which cared for infants left homeless. The babies on the second floor of the orphanage seemed to be doing quite well, while the babies on the first and third floors were sickly and dying.

The doctors could not understand why the infants on the second floor were thriving. The food and hygienic routines were the same on all the floors.

After their investigations led nowhere, it was brought to the attention of the doctors that an old cleaning lady was to be dismissed from her job on the second floor because she was ignoring her duties. Instead of washing the floors during the midnight shift, she left her work so that she could soothe the crying babies. This old cleaning lady had provided the infants with something which was just as necessary to their total development as food and cleanliness. Without touch, the babies were dying; with it they survived.

To deprive a child of touch conveys to him that he really is not worth very much. When you touch another person, you are telling him you care, that you like him. He means something to you. Touch is the silent language of love.

At the moment of your touch the other person is made to feel that he is the only person in your life. He has a feeling of exclusiveness which is the beginning stage of love. A touch says, "At this time, you are the only one who matters to me."

Dr. Virginia Satir, a social scientist in Menlo Park, California and a member of the American Orthopsychiatric Association, believes that hugging transfers energy and gives an emotional boost.

The skin is the largest organ we have, and it needs a great deal of care. A hug can cover a lot of skin area and gives the message that you care. A hug is also a form of communication. It means that you are open to giving and receiving. It enables you to tell another person how you feel about him. The nicest thing about a hug is that you usually can't give one without getting one. (from a speech)

She suggests that the average person needs four hugs a day for survival, eight for maintenance, and twelve for growth.

In a normal family situation, it is not difficult to cuddle and love a baby. But something begins to happen as that baby makes the progression from a toddler to school-age child, and eventually into a teenager. As the child grows older the touching usually diminishes.

Children never outgrow the need to be touched. And adults never outgrow it either. Our bodies cry out for it, especially in a society where touching is greatly repressed.

In most homes, the need for touch is great. We need this constant contact with one another as a demonstration of caring.

When it is not there we lose something in communication and in the awareness of other persons as special. That deep-seated hunger within us cries out to the world: "Touch me. Tell me I'm worth something."

There is no better way to express to your children how very special they are than by touching them. At the point of contact, love is expressed and self-worth is established. "I am someone special because another person took the time to touch me."

Peanut Butter Sandwiches and Oreo Cookies

Sometimes we need to structure excuses for loving and touching one another. As children grow older, they tend to shy away from physical expressions of love. Boys think it is "dumb" and feel embarrassed when Mom kisses them good-bye or Dad wants to hug them.

Warren and I have always touched our children a lot, and we became concerned when we saw them shying away from it. So we devised a technique of making "Peanut butter and jelly sandwiches" and "Oreo cookies," to give us an excuse for hugging and loving each child.

When our children were very young, they would eagerly love us with everything they had. As they grew up, we would have to chase them around the kitchen table in order to get a good hug.

Now, instead of asking for a hug we just announce, "Oreo cookie time." This means that one of our children is going to receive a hug. Since no one knows who it is they all scurry. When we catch one of them in our grasp, Warren becomes one part of the cookie, I become the other side, and whoever is in the middle gets to be the creme. A three-way body hug happens, with giggles coming from the child in the middle. If we want to get four people in a hug, we call, "Peanut butter and jelly sandwich time." Dad is one slice of bread, I'm the other, and the two kids in the middle are the peanut butter and jelly.

We have learned to love this little game. Even our older children have accepted their parents' crazy tactics and, despite much squirming and giggling, give in to being touched and held. This has become such a tradition around our home that people visiting us have this ritual explained to them. Grandpa and Grandma have been made into "Oreo cookies" as well as some of our friends. I love being in the middle too. Everyone else also admits how good it feels.

Love Bumps, Pats, and Squeezes

Each time your small children pass by you, try to touch them. Pat their little bottoms softly, ruffle their hair, or pat their heads. Take their face gently into your hands, establish eye contact, and give them a kiss on the cheek. Tell them that you love them. Tickle their arms and legs lightly. They will love the sensation which this gives.

Sidney B. Simon in his book *Caring, Feeling, Touching* recommends that arm rubs are a good way of touching. What takes place in an arm rub is "a gentle pressing of the arm from the wrist up to the shoulder." Sometimes this can take the form of gentle tickling. While watching TV with your children, try this particular technique of touching.

Children also enjoy back and neck rubs. These should be given periodically especially to children who have difficulty falling asleep.

To get my children up in the morning for school, I would gently rub their back and say, "Come on you sleepyhead, it's time to get up." They would wiggle and a little smile would begin to appear on their faces, and the back rub would eventually turn into a tickling match.

Use every available opportunity to touch your children. Don't stop just because they are getting older. The one who runs the hardest from touch is usually the one who needs it the most. Be persistent. In subtle ways express your love. Tell them you care, that they are special. Pat them on the head; touch their arms; squeeze their hands in yours. They will receive the message loud and clear.

Blessing Our Children

The touch of God's blessing upon your children is a way of making them feel special. At the point of physical contact, the love of God can be conveyed to people. I believe that God uses our hands to give others His special touch. He lives inside of me and therefore, I am His representative. Through me, His love reaches out to others.

I try not to let a day go by without bestowing a blessing on my children. As they leave for school in the morning, a kiss and a "God be with you today" goes with them. Before they go to sleep, I give them a hug and a "God bless you tonight while you sleep." As they embark on a difficult task, I remind them that I will be asking God to bless them during it.

The child's first day back to school is an opportunity for us as a family to ask the blessings of God on the new school year. Warren usually does this the morning of that first day.

Sometimes mornings are so busy that the time of blessing is not ministered verbally to my children. Time seems to get away from me. As I go through my day, little prayers of blessing go before the throne of God. I try to remember the time when they will be encountering that big exam or the tryout for a particular sport. "Lord, bless them right now as they are. . ."

Love Notes

Have you ever thought of writing your child a little note and placing it in his lunch? It doesn't have to be a "mushy" one. My boys would be terribly embarrassed if that happened. I have written notes to my children telling them that they are thought of during the day. Sometimes a "happy face" is drawn with the words, "Have a good day." John received one such note and was the envy of his classmates. He was so proud and felt special.

Kisses in a Pocket

Sometimes little ones have a difficult time being separated from their mothers. They need constant reminders that their mothers still love them and will return. One mother found a solution in helping her child remember that she loved him. On leaving her child for the day, she took a piece of Kleenex, blotted her lipstick on it, folded it into a little square, and placed it in her child's pocket. "This is to remind you that Mommy loves you a whole lot," she said. "When you feel lonely, remember that you have my kiss in your pocket."

The woman who was caring for this child during the hours of separation told the mother that her child would often check his pocket to look at the kiss that was there. It comforted him to know that part of his mother was with him.

Their Birth

Every child loves to hear over and over again the incidents which accompanied his birth. What he is really hearing is that the day was something special in the life of the family. He was anticipated, and waited for. There was much planning associated with his arrival.

We often go into great detail with each one of our children in relating the circumstances which took place before and after they were born. As old as they are, they still like hearing it as much as we enjoy telling it.

It begins with the explanation of how much we desired to have children. Their conception is explained as a miracle which God performed in Mommy. Daddy and Mommy loved each other, and children were a natural outcome of that love.

They were special even before they were born. As God was developing their inward parts (Psalm 139), His hand was on them. He knew all about them at that time—their name, what they would look like, what their purpose in life was going to be.

We tell them how they would kick inside of me to let me know that they would soon be arriving, and that I loved them even before they were a visible part of our family.

We describe their birth, with the funny incidents of trying to get to the hospital on time. Johnny and Elisabeth were born in New Guinea, where there were mountains to climb, plane trips to the hospital, and dangerous jeep rides over bumpy roads.

The excitement builds as we approach the birth. We loved them even though they were all wrinkly, and had heads which were long and out of shape. We didn't have to think twice about keeping them.

They want to hear more and more because it is about them. They are special. So we talk about those early toddler years and the mischievous, funny things they got into. Each child was different and gave us joy in a way which was unique only to him.

The Meaning of Their Names

When I was a little girl, my mother explained to me that Elise means "consecrated to God." What an impact that made on me! I was a person who was dedicated to God.

Several years ago, Warren and I looked into the meanings of the names of our children and other family members. Proverbs 22:1 says, "A good name is to be more desired than great riches." We wanted each one to know the meaning of his name and the spiritual significance attached to it. Our children's names, with their secular and spiritual meanings, are now displayed in our kitchen on wooden plaques as a daily reminder.

Paul was not too thrilled when he found out his name meant "small" or "little." I wondered what spiritual significance could be put on such a meaning. With the help of a concordance, I came across the following Bible verse which gave Paul a motto to live by! "If you have faith as a mustard seed, you shall say to this mountain, 'Move from here to there,' and it shall move;

and nothing shall be impossible to you" (Matthew 17:20). God knows each of our children by name. We want them to know that they are special to Him.

A Day for Someone Special
In large families a child may get lost in the crowd. He is remembered on his birthday, but the rest of the year he is just another member of the family.

Time needs to be taken from busy routines to show children how very special they are. This particular tradition was one we practiced when our children were younger, and they have not forgotten it.

Each Friday was a special day for somebody. We usually started with the youngest child, only because he lacked patience in having to wait for his day.

The day would begin with a special wake-up time. I would enter his room, rub his back, and whisper in his ear, "Today is Johnny's Day. Let's get up so we can enjoy every minute of it." That day John would be "King Bee." He would not have to do any work around the house, since his chores were done by his brothers and sister. He would not even have to make his bed. He chose the menu for the evening meal. Sometimes I would shudder as he picked out his favorite foods—Cheerios and hamburgers, with ice cream for dessert.

Another privilege given that day was the honor of sitting in Daddy's chair. He did not have to say "King's-X" to reserve it. It was his for the entire day.

With some regulating from Mom he was allowed to watch his favorite TV programs. In a family of four children and one TV, squabbles sometimes erupt over who is going to watch what program. On special days, we didn't have this problem.

Each child anticipated his day for weeks ahead. When it finally came, he could hardly contain himself. During the hours he was away at school he thought about coming home.

When he arrived home, there was a sign on the door which read: "Today is Johnny's Day." He was so excited. As Paul and David grew older, the sign had to go. They claimed they would be embarrassed if any of their neighborhood friends saw it. Later, they found that their friends were really envious of what was going on.

At supper the special child would receive a crown to wear and would be the first one served. All through the meal he was told only good things about himself. Telling him about his birth was also part of the ritual. At the end of the meal a special prayer of blessing was given for the child of the day.

Each week honored a different person. Even Mom and Dad were included.

Planning a day each week for one person in the family was a lot of work. Special food needed to be bought and prepared. Time needed to be spent with the child of the day. But the time spent created fond memories for our family.

At times I would like to return to this tradition. Even with our children as old as they are, I know they would still enjoy it. I suppose the signs, crowns, and some other things would have to go; but the awareness that they are someone special would still be there.

Scheduling is the big problem when children get older. It is important to build memories when your children are young and at home. There will not be time later.

God Loves You and So Do I

One of the exercises which I performed with my small children on a regular basis reminded them of our love and God's love. We would talk about all the people who love them. "Mommy loves you, Daddy loves you, Paul, David, and Elisabeth love you, Johnny." Then other relatives or friends might be mentioned. "But do you know who loves you best of all? Very best of all, Jesus loves you."

This routine was a natural part of their day. Accompanied with lots of hugs and kisses, they were assured of their family's love and the love of God. John 3:16 is a Bible verse which our young children learned. In the place of "world," sometimes we would say, "God so loved John."

There are many different ways we can express to our children that they are special to us and to God. One mother had a difficult time dealing with her son. He was diagnosed as hyperkinetic, and had real behavior problems at school and home. As a result, she found it difficult to see anything for which she could praise him. She admitted that at times she just didn't like him. Her days were filled with antagonism and quarreling. Trying to find something good about him was next to impossible, until she took it to the Lord in prayer. She knew her boy was special to God, and that He would show her how to handle this situation.

This boy loved to make up stories, and she never knew when he was telling the truth. When God showed her that he possessed a vivid imagination with the potential of becoming extremely creative, she knew she could use this as a starting point in finding something good about him.

One day she complimented him on the "creative" story he had just told her. Of course, he was shocked at her response, since he expected her to accuse him of lying. She encouraged him to make up another story for her, and she listened with rapt attention. The boy was in his glory. As she held him on her lap and took time to listen, she began to see changes take place. He was learning to use his imagination in a creative way. Later, he became quite adept at writing and telling stories.

A change began to take place in their life together as mother and child touched more, as she listened to him, and began to praise him for specific good points in his life.

A little extra time of loving can do so much for all of us. Any child growing up in a loving environment will know that he is special.

Have you been making your children feel special? With God's help you can find many creative ways to express your love. This legacy of specialness is worth more than any material gain you can provide for your children.

8
Traditions–
Family Legacy

"You mean we are not going to have Easter baskets this year? How could you do this to us? It's tradition!" That's what we heard when we informed our children that this year the Easter basket ritual would be canceled. Our family's dream of going to the Holy Land had finally come true. We were leaving the day after Easter to spend ten glorious days in Jordan, Israel, and Egypt. To me it seemed foolish to spend money on the traditional Easter candy, fuzzy chickens, bunnies, and other favors which were all part of the Easter morning tradition. It just didn't fit in with my busy schedule of packing, and with the reality that in a few days we would be walking in the footsteps of Jesus.

"After all," I thought, "my children are no longer toddlers. They have reached the so-called 'sophisticated' teenage years, and surely should be able to understand my viewpoint." But instead of their understanding, I had a minirebellion on my hands.

It didn't make any difference how old they were. My teenagers were wallowing in self-pity. It was not easy for them to part with a tradition which had been part of their lives ever since they were babies. They loved the excitement of the night before Easter, and the anticipation of finding their carefully hidden baskets. Often I would hear them discussing if Mom and Dad would be able to find new hiding places. After all, how many more could there be?

Each year we did manage to surprise them. The entire house became territory for their search. One year we hid David's basket so well he didn't find it until that afternoon. Frustrated, he finally asked us to give him "hot and cold" clues, which according to the other children was a last resort.

I remember this same tradition in my own home as a child. I was 21 and married before my own mother stopped giving me a basket on Easter morning. Even as a young adult, I felt something inside—a return to my childhood, a stirring of the little girl still inside of me. It was something good and right. It made me feel loved, cared for, and appreciated.

The Importance of Traditions

Through this Easter basket incident, I was reminded again of how very important the creating of traditions and the resulting memories have been to our children. They weren't nearly as interested in the candy and the goodies as in the fun, excitement, and love which had been a part of this family ritual each year.

An article published in the *Detroit News* (December 23, 1981) entitled "Holiday Rituals: A Family Affair," discusses the importance of establishing family traditions.

Social scientists believe that such rites within the family are important because they make each individual aware of being a part of a common group and heritage.

"Holiday traditions encourage family members to intensify their interaction with—and renew their commitment to—each other," says Dr. Thomas J. Powell, professor of social work at the University of Michigan.

"Traditions help people reach out to each other with a feeling of 'Let's do something and get outside ourselves.' "

They also establish a "collective uniqueness, a certain stability and continuity in a family," adds Dr. J. Ross Eshleman, chairman of Wayne State University's sociology department.

"They help a person reassess his values in terms of himself and in terms of his own identity within the family."

Jay Schvandveldt, a sociologist at Utah State University who has studied the rituals of hundreds of families, points out that families with the strongest ties have the most rituals.

They are important not so much for whatever is actually said or done, but for the results they yield—the sense of "we-ness" that grows out of shared experiences, and the feeling of "rightness" that comes from its repetition. More than anything else, the ritual is a symbol of how family members feel about one another. "The Joy of Family Rituals," *McCall's,* December 1981.

The traditions we build within the family are some of the best gifts we give to our children. They become ways in which a family plays together and communicates love. A family rich in tradition is a family which longs to be with one another. Traditions become the binding factor which draws the family together even after the children have established families of their own.

The Celebrating Family

Both my husband and I consider it a blessing to have grown up in homes strong in traditions. In the early years of our marriage the oneness which we felt with our own families caused a few arguments between us. Christmas would come and the big decision would have to be made about where we would be spending Christmas Eve and the succeeding holidays. I could not picture Christmas any other place but at my home. All the rituals associated with it made my heart long to be there. But Warren felt exactly the same way about his family.

Our first Christmas in New Guinea, far from family and friends, had to be one of the loneliest for us. No Christmas programs to attend, no turkey dinner fixed by one of our mothers, no exchange of gifts, no cookie baking, and no decorating. All I could picture was our family at home going through the many treasured rituals associated with the Christmas celebration—and we were separated from it all. I would have given almost anything that lonely night to fly those 12,000 miles to my home.

As our little family grew, we began to establish traditions of our own. We adjusted to our new environment, to being away from family. There still is a twinge of longing in me to return to the traditions of my childhood, but much stronger is the joy of our own family becoming grounded in traditions of our own. Over the years we have become a celebrating family.

The day is fast approaching when our children will be leaving the secure nest of the home. Will the celebrating we have done in their early years be the drawing force which will beckon them home? My prayer is that they will always want to return home; but even more, that the celebrating which we have done will be continued within their own families, as a precious legacy which they have inherited.

If ever there was a need for family celebration, it is today. The family which celebrates is bound close to each other in a sense of unity which sociologists find missing in so many families. A celebrating family is a happy one; they are celebrating the very act of living.

In our growing family of four small children we learned to use every excuse to celebrate. The losing of a first tooth, the first day of school, the first day of vacation from school, report cards, band concerts. Basketball, baseball, and soccer games became natural excuses for some type of party. A stop at the local root beer stand, pizza parlor, or just buying a gallon of our favorite ice cream, whipping cream, and topping were some of the ways we found of commemorating these events.

Our yearly fishing vacation was always preceded by a tradition which Elisabeth and I still find hard to appreciate. We have learned to endure it and realize that our vacation would not be the same without it. Weeks before the day of departure, Dad and the boys take over the family room. Scattered everywhere are tackle boxes, fishing reels and line, all types of lures, and artificial bait. The tradition begins by emptying the tackle boxes and examining each item for defects. A thorough cleaning takes place. Such care is taken to make each silver spoon lure shine its brightest. A list is then compiled of the many items needed in order to make this fishing trip the most successful one ever.

As our men seriously pursue this task, Elisabeth and I listen to fish stories from years past. Warren pulls out a lure and tells us all about the time "illusive George" hit on it. "He must have been at least 25 pounds," he says excitedly, as the boys all nod in agreement.

What precious moments for Warren to share with his boys. Their eyes are like saucers as they sit on the floor at his feet, in wonder at their father's knowledge of catching fish.

Despite our inability to understand the seriousness at which the men in our family pursue this task, we do understand that it is part of a family ritual. Even after our teasing about their fish stories, Liz and I are always invited for the grand finale of this tradition—a ride to the local fishing shop to purchase the much needed equipment to complete their tackle boxes.

The secular traditions we celebrate as a family are important to us. Through them fond memories have been implanted in the minds of our children. But of far more importance and greater significance has been the building of family love and unity. We have established roots that will be nurtured, pruned, adapted, and passed on to future generations.

The celebrating of secular traditions is necessary in any

family, but of greater importance is the establishing of spiritual traditions. It is obvious from the number of young people joining cults, and from the number of older people within our churches who flock to ritualistic encounter groups, that there is need for spiritual celebration.

Through spiritual traditions children learn how to experience and express their faith. They interact with family members and in so doing, interact with God's love.

Signs and Symbols

Children need tangible evidence, things they can feel and see, experiences which excite their emotions.

When I taught school, I was very aware of the importance of visual aids or object lessons. I could tell the children something over and over again, but until I got their attention with the use of an object, it just did not sink in. Traditions are much like visual aids.

In his book *The Christian Family,* Larry Christenson has this to say about the use of symbols or visual aids: "A symbol can express the truth more simply and more profoundly than mere words. Christian symbols are spiritual windows through which God's truth can shine." Symbols are silent teachers, expressing visually what would take many words to explain.

God knows we need symbols to remind us of His love and to help us in our celebrating. When the Children of Israel crossed the Jordan River, God used a visual aid to illustrate His promise:

And Joshua said to them, "Cross again to the ark of the Lord your God into the middle of the Jordan, and each of you take up a stone on his shoulder, according to the number of the tribes of the sons of Israel.

"Let this be a sign among you, so that when your children ask later, saying, 'What do these stones mean to you?' Then you shall say to them, 'Because the waters of the Jordan were cut off before the ark of the covenant of the

Lord; when it crossed the Jordan, the waters of the Jordan were cut off.' So these stones shall become a memorial to the sons of Israel forever" (Joshua 4:5–7).

The Israelite nation was rich in traditions, many of which had been ordained by God Himself. The killing of the unblemished lamb at Passover, the blood over the doorposts, the cleansing of leaven from each home, the eating of the Passover meal, were all traditions ordained by God for a purpose.

And it shall serve as a sign to you on your hand, and as a reminder on your forehead, that the Law of the Lord may be in your mouth; for with a powerful hand the Lord brought you out of Egypt.

And it shall be when your son asks you in time to come, saying, "What is this?" then you shall say to him, "With a powerful hand the Lord brought us out of Egypt, from the house of slavery" (Exodus 13:9, 14).

In Deuteronomy 6:7–9 we are commanded to teach our children through physical reminders:

And you shall teach them diligently to your sons and shall talk of them when you sit in your house and when you walk by the way and when you lie down and when you rise up.

And you shall bind them as a sign on your hand and they shall be as frontals on your forehead.

And you shall write them on the doorposts of your house and on your gates.

In a practicing Jewish home, religious traditions and symbols reinforce to the family where they have come from and who their God is. One such symbol is a small rectangular box placed on the doorpost of an Orthodox Jewish home. Enclosed in the box is the great Shema of Deuteronomy 6:4–9 which begins, "Hear, O Israel: The Lord our God is one Lord."

As you pass through the doorway of the home you are to touch this box as a reminder that the Lord God Jehovah is the God of this particular house; that He is our God and that He is

One! How beautiful to be continually reminded of God's presence.

The core of any religious tradition should be a heart relationship of love toward God. Without this the tradition is meaningless in our spiritual lives. Jesus was quite emphatic about this when He admonished the scribes and Pharisees about how they kept the traditions. His disappointment was not in the traditions, but that the Pharisees had made them an end in themselves for good works, rather than a means for expressing their love for God. "This people draw near with their words and honor Me with their lip service, but they remove their hearts far from Me, and their reverence for Me consists of traditions learned by rote" (Isaiah 29:13).

Begin To Celebrate

Not all families are celebrating families. The complexion of many family groups is one of shyness, with feelings of hesitancy and self-consciousness at expressing their feelings. If you are not a celebrating family, but desire to be one, remember that God works with our desires. When we seek Him first, He is more than willing to provide the necessary avenues for fulfilling those desires which are according to His will. It will not be easy at first, but with a little perseverance it can be done. In the beginning you may feel self-conscious, but your children will sense your love and enthusiasm as you make your early attempts at establishing spiritual traditions.

Start simply. Explain to your children what you are planning to do and why you are doing it. If they are old enough, explain to them the importance of celebrating together as a family. If you know a celebrating family, ask them to help you get started. Whatever you do, don't put it off until your children are older.

If you have already learned the art of celebrating on a secular level, you will probably have little difficulty in moving to spiritual celebrations.

One of the best ways to begin to celebrate spiritually within the family context is by using religious holidays. In the next pages I will be sharing with you some of the many ways we have celebrated different religious holidays.

Christmas

The Christmas season is an easy time to begin spiritual family traditions. Our celebration usually starts four weeks before Christmas. This four-week period is called Advent, which means "coming." On that first Sunday in Advent we have the traditional lighting of the first candle in our Advent wreath. Each week we light another candle. Each day during the lighting of the candles, a Scripture verse is read from our Advent calendar.

Our Advent wreath is made up of five candles—three purple, one pink, and one white candle which is set in the center. The purple candles represent humility and repentance, the turning away from sin and preparing our hearts and lives for the Second Coming of our Lord Jesus. They also remind us that the joy of Christmas is possible only when we acknowledge our sinfulness before God and accept the forgiveness we receive through His Son Jesus. The candles are set in a circular spray of evergreens which symbolize the life found in Christ. Despite the drabness of nature during winter, the evergreen continues to be green. The circle represents our oneness in Christ.

The lighting of the candles is symbolic of the coming of Jesus, the living Light of the World. The act of lighting one candle each week tells of the increasing brightness of Christ as we await His coming.

On Christmas Eve all four candles are lit plus the white one which signifies the birth of Christ. Some families use a small manger with the Baby Jesus in it, instead of the white candle.

• Another Advent tradition is "the filling of the Advent Crib." This too uses an Advent calendar to provide the family a daily schedule of Scripture readings.

The family working together constructs a manger out of cardboard or plywood, and then buys some straw. A small doll wrapped in a blanket, symbolizing the Baby Jesus, is going to occupy the manger, after it is made ready for Him.

Every day during the Advent season, after the Bible verse has been read from the Advent calendar, each member of the family takes a piece of straw and places it in the manger. This represents the preparation of our hearts for the coming of Jesus as our King. Just as we want to make the bed nice and soft for the Baby Jesus, so we want our hearts to be prepared to receive Jesus and His love.

• Another tradition in our home has to do with decorating our Christmas tree. Through the years we have received many handmade ornaments from dear friends. The children also have made ornaments for us which we love. I call our Christmas tree our "treasure tree" because it is filled with many memories of special people. As we place each ornament on the tree, we are reminded of the person who gave it to us. An informal prayer of blessing is spoken, such as "God bless the Scotts this Christmas." Often we relate some funny incident or unique trait about that person. It is a happy time and once again is building memories and love.

Because of the commercialism which is associated with Christmas, we have tried to emphasize to our children that foremost in our minds should be the celebration of the birthday of Jesus. As I was growing up, the lights on our Christmas tree were never lit until Christmas Eve. The lighting of the Christmas tree was our way of lighting the candles for Jesus' birthday.

• If you have small children, you might like to buy a small Nativity scene for each child in the family. It need not be an expensive one but should have movable figures. Our children would play for hours each Christmas season, arranging and rearranging these figures. Often I would hear them telling the Christmas story to each other.

Easter

The Easter season is also an excellent time to begin traditions within the family. Our preparation begins 40 days before Easter on Ash Wednesday, the first day of a time of sincere repentance and meditation on the suffering and death of our Lord Jesus. It is a time of particular concentration on prayer, reading of the Scriptures, and desire to be led by the Holy Spirit. It is not that these things should only be done during Lent, but that we are reminded during this season how we fail in living for Christ. Lent is a call to greater commitment in the believer's life.

In our family we encourage each person to give something up during Lent as a constant reminder of the sacrifice which Jesus had to make for us. If our children have difficulty in doing this, we encourage, as an alternative, for them to give something *to* Jesus—such as more time spent in prayer, extra money they might have saved and would like to give to a missionary, kind acts to others, and service to their church.

• The Lenten season offers great opportunity for the family to learn how to pray together. If you are not a praying family, this is an excellent time to teach your children about prayer.

Begin slowly and simply. When they sit in their high chairs or around the table for their morning snack, explain to them that you are all going to fold your hands and thank Jesus for your food.

Their prayers need not be long or involved. You may be amazed at how honest and sincere they are. "God, please bless my Cheerios and help Elisabeth not to cry" is said straight from the heart.

In teaching your children how to pray, place before them a picture of a smiling Jesus who is happy that they want to talk to Him. You can say that He loves them and gets lonesome for them when they don't take the time to pray. He enjoys listening to them and never gets tired of hearing their prayers.

As you progress from simple mealtime prayers, you will be

finding they will want to pray for other things and at other times. Before your children go to sleep you can say a prayer with them or have them say their own. Cuddle with them as you pray, holding them in your arms or kneeling beside their bed with them. They will enjoy the closeness and these will be special moments for you also.

What are some of the things you could encourage your children to pray about? They are not interested in the world situation or even about most things going on in their church. But they are totally involved with their family, their pets, lost toys, sick friends, and skinned elbows.

Another good opportunity for teaching children to pray for others is something which my mother did with us. Each time we would hear a siren she would say, "OK, children, pray in your hearts for the fireman, the policeman, the ambulance driver, and anyone who might be hurt in the fire or accident. Ask God to bless them and take care of them, even though you do not know who they are." This type of praying has carried over into the prayer life of our children.

The Lenten season is an excellent time for you and your children to learn Bible verses about prayer. If you learn just one Bible verse each week, you will soon have a storehouse of Bible verses in your hearts. One which we used is Jeremiah 33:3: "Call unto Me and I will answer thee and show thee great and mighty things that thou knowest not." We called it God's telephone number.

Your refrigerator is a good place to post the Bible verse for the week. It is there right in front of you as a daily reminder.

• As a child I remember the Lenten season being a time of fasting. Even though we were Protestant, Fridays were set aside as fasting days.

Holy Week, beginning with Palm Sunday, is a time of personal reflection in our home, for during it our focal point is the suffering of our Lord Jesus Christ. Maundy Thursday is the day we commemorate the instituting of the Lord's Supper with the disciples.

Good Friday is a day my children will always remember. They refer to it as "the time of quiet." Once again memories return to me of this special day in my childhood home. We were not allowed to listen to the radio or TV, play any musical instruments, or talk loudly. It was a day of fasting, keeping quiet, and attending church. It was all done with the purpose of constantly reminding us of the suffering of Jesus on the cross for our sins.

We have carried this tradition of quietness over to our own home. It has not always been an easy one for our children to accept. No one likes to be quiet for an entire day. But our children have and still do cooperate.

• On Easter morning we use the traditional Easter greeting with each other. My husband is usually the first one up and greets me with, "Elise, it is Easter morning. Jesus is risen!" To which I respond, "Hallelujah, He is risen indeed!" We then awaken each child in the same manner.

• Pentecost and Ascension Day are church holidays which many of us tend to forget. But passing by them without notice deprives us of another chance to grow in Christ and to celebrate.

Be sure to read the biblical accounts to your children. On Ascension Day I used to take my children outside and have them lie on the grass and look at the clouds. These are a constant reminder to us of the coming again of our Lord Jesus Christ in glory. Just as Jesus ascended into the clouds, so His second coming will be through the clouds. (See Acts 1:9–11; 1 Thessalonians 4:16–17.)

As a child I often wondered why Jesus had to leave this earth. It didn't make much sense to me. I would have loved to have Him walk and talk with me in a physical way. It wasn't until many years later, through one of Warren's sermons, that I really understood why Jesus had to return home to His heavenly Father.

Warren used a simple illustration from his own childhood which explained so clearly the importance of the Ascension. He recounted from his past how he would often disobey his father and mother. There were plenty of city parks at which to play ball, but Warren and his boyfriends decided it was too much trouble to walk to them. Instead, they chose to play in the street in front of their homes, hoping they could finish a game without breaking any windows. Warren was one of the bigger boys and one of the best hitters. One day his turn at bat sent a baseball sailing through a neighbor's window. At the sound of the crash everyone ran and hid. Warren knew what the penalty was—it wasn't the first time this had happened. The size of his father's hand and also the dwindling economy of his piggy bank told him he was in for trouble.

Soon the word was out that Warren was responsible for the broken window. Afraid to go home, he hid in a vacant lot, hoping not to be found by anyone. Soon he heard his father calling for him to return home. How he wished someone would be kind enough to take his place. He wished someone would go to his father and say, "Don't punish Warren. He is sorry for what he did. I will pay for the broken window."

Many years later it dawned on Warren that this incident illustrated why Jesus had to ascend into heaven and be with His heavenly Father. We are all guilty of "broken windows" in our lives. Sin and its judgment plague us constantly. Jesus is the One who goes to our heavenly Father to plead our case. Because of what Jesus has done through His death on the cross, our debt is paid in full. We can stand blameless before our heavenly Father. Jesus takes us by the hand to God, and says, "Look, Father, Bob is sorry for what he has done. I have paid the price for his sins. Accept him."

Other Special Days

There are many holidays which can be celebrated in both a secular and spiritual way. Be sure to go to your public library and read about people such as St. Patrick and St. Valentine. You will discover a wealth of information about these men and their love for God. St. Patrick was a courageous missionary. Along with other celebration, St. Patrick's Day can include an emphasis on the importance of foreign missions. Read to your children the Great Commission, Matthew 28:19–20, which Jesus gave to His disciples and to us as well.

• Flag Day, the Fourth of July, and Memorial Day can be explained to children from a spiritual and patriotic point of view. Our country and the freedom we possess are gifts from God. Patriotism needs to be cultivated in the lives of children. Teach your children to respect flag and country and the authority which is placed over us. Read Romans 13:1–7 to them and explain that we need to honor those in authority.

• Most Christians tend to shy away from establishing spiritual traditions around Halloween. So much of the satanic is associated with Halloween that we tend to forget that we can use this holiday as an opportunity to be a blessing to our neighbors. Yet many families have turned this evening into a time of witnessing the love of Christ to the children of the neighborhood.

The word *Halloween* really means "holy evening." In the eighth century, Gregory II set aside November 1 as All Saints Day, to honor and remember the lives and examples of faithful Christians who are now with Christ. The night before November 1 was used as a Hallowed Eve to prepare for the meaning of the coming holy day.

In our family we enjoy this evening, and see it as an opportunity to love the children in our neighborhood. I dress up in some type of funny costume. Even our dog gets into the act with a big bow tied around her neck. Our treat to each child includes pennies, a treat, and a tract which tells them the salvation story.

As we work on this project, we are praying that through our efforts some child will come to know Jesus.

Instead of carving a pumpkin with the traditional jack-o-lantern face, we carve a cross into the pumpkin, and then light a candle inside. Many of the children who come to our home comment on how beautiful our pumpkin is. As they talk to us, we explain to them that Jesus is the Light of the World and that He has won the victory over the darkness of death, sin, and the devil.

There is no other night of the year when we have contact with so many neighborhood children. As a family we take advantage of such a time to extend the love of Christ to them.

The opportunities for spiritual celebration are almost endless. I have shared with you only a few occasions for establishing traditions. As you consider your family, you will add to the list. Don't limit yourself to holidays, but use every possible time to celebrate the presence of Christ within your home.

9
Wise
Building

After my sister Cindy read several chapters of this manuscript, she called me long distance. So many things I wrote about brought back memories from our childhood. What amazed her was that even though we had raised our children in different parts of the world, our attitudes toward childrearing were almost identical. We both used many of the same methods which our mother had used with us.

When my mother read the manuscript, she said, "Why, these are some of the same things Grandma did with me when I was a child." My mother also had an excellent model on which to base her mothering. Grandma radiated to my mother the same love of Jesus that was in my home as a little child. Now Cindy and I are passing to the fourth generation the blessings of a godly heritage.

Maybe your childhood experience was not one you would like to pass on to your children. God can heal the hurts, and cause you to be the first generation of godly mothers, as you pass on to your children the blessing of growing up in a Christian environment.

We mothers are in the process of building for future generations. A mother who loves Jesus, and longs to be like Him in every respect, has the ability to transform any ordinary home into the very dwelling place of God. Her home becomes a place where Jesus lives and loves. In such an environment, His presence can be felt at every turn.

To live the pure and holy life within the confines of your home, among people who know you best, is one of the most difficult tasks you will ever do. It is easy to exhibit Christian love and virtue outside the home. Volunteer work has its rewards, for people see you as self-sacrificing and giving. Your willingness to serve and your smiling face are always welcome by others who can hardly picture you scowling or angry. But then, they don't live with you on a day-by-day basis. They see you at your best, and don't experience any ups and downs of your 28-day cycle.

It is not easy to treat people in your home with as much thoughtfulness and gratitude as you do those who are just acquaintances. Yet home is the place where you are being conformed day by day into the very image of Jesus Christ. God uses the people in your home to teach you how to react in the same way Jesus reacted. You will learn the very qualities of Jesus Christ, and also, how often you fall short of the glory of God. In your home you are being prepared for service in the kingdom of God. As you daily trust in Jesus, the things which you learn from the Holy Spirit are then conveyed to your children. These everyday teachings can influence their entire lives for God.

King David wrote, "I will walk within my house in the integrity of my heart" (Psalm 101:2). Even though he was king over Israel and recognized outside his home as someone to be honored and respected, in his own home he desired to walk uprightly, with a pure heart. It is difficult to take on the role of a servant in your home, to exhibit an attitude of humility. This is something God can work in you, as He causes your speech and actions to give glory to Him in every situation.

The example which mothers set in the home produces its atmosphere or tone, so that a sense of order and love, and an air of peacefulness permeate every space within a house.

The atmosphere of a home has little to do with its physical appearance. I admire homes which are beautifully decorated and homes which are immaculate, everything in its proper place. I believe that God wants us to care for our homes and make them into places which are pleasing to others. But the physical appearance of a home does not govern the presence of God. This comes about only as the Holy Spirit works within the lives of the people who live there.

The carpeting may be worn and the drapes faded from the sun. There may be dishes in the kitchen sink, or toys scattered on the floor, and yet there still can be a conscious feeling of something special present. People entering such a home find themselves feeling welcome, loved, and accepted. This type of home becomes a refuge for anyone who has experienced the harshness of life and the unkind world of sin.

What makes a home feel so warm and loving? And how can we as mothers produce this in our daily physical surroundings? When a mother is happy and content with her life, the home generates this feeling. When she is living a life of bitterness, resentment, and anger, these feelings fill a house with discord and unrest.

I know it is easy to blame other factors in your home for the state of unrest. Many women would like to put the blame on a husband, a mother-in-law, a child, or their physical surroundings. But blaming someone or something else for our problems is a trap. God wants us to take a good look at ourselves, to see what changes need to take place in our own lives.

The writer of the Proverbs said:
Better is a dish of vegetables where love is,
Than a fattened ox and hatred with it (15:17).
Better is a dry morsel and quietness with it

Than a house full of feasting with strife (17:1).
It is better to live in the corner of a roof,
Than in a house shared with a contentious woman (21:9).
A constant dripping on a day of steady rain
And a contentious woman are alike;
He who would restrain her restrains the wind,
And grasps oil with his right hand (27:15–16).
It is better to live in a desert land,
Than with a contentious and vexing woman (21:19).

Where there is bitterness or strife in the lives of the adults, a home will be toned by restlessness and uneasiness. The woman described in Proverbs is called "contentious and vexing." This type of woman causes men and children to prefer the corner of an attic or a desert place to a lovely home shared with her. Other words which could be used to describe her are: combative, belligerent, warlike, quarrelsome, spiteful, malicious, hateful, and irritating.

I certainly don't want to be described that way. Yet there have been times when I have fallen into the trap of making life miserable for other family members, by being that "contentious, vexing" woman.

When that happens, I see a difference in my home. My children would rather not be around me. Frustration builds in their lives and their behavior begins to demonstrate what they feel inside. My husband would rather work late at his office than be in the presence of a moody wife who is ready for battle with anyone who gets in her way.

If my home were the most elegant in town, it wouldn't mean much if love were not present in my life and actions. A mother dedicated to herself and what she wants will produce an unpleasant atmosphere in the home. But a mother under the control of the Holy Spirit will become the kind of woman described in Proverbs 31. "She opens her mouth in wisdom, and the teaching of kindness is on her tongue" (v. 26).

I want my home to be filled with love, joy, and peace. I want people to sense something special when they enter, to feel the presence of Jesus. Each day I ask God to help me live according to His will, especially in my home.

By Late Afternoon

Let's look at an average day in your life. It may include cleaning, laundry, running errands, doctors' appointments, neighbors dropping in for coffee, a Bible study at church, volunteer service at your children's school or in the community, gardening or decorating or sewing. By late afternoon you are exhausted and would like to relax, only to realize that supper is just around the corner. Frustration builds. You are tired and to complicate things, you remember that you forgot to defrost the meat.

Suppertime, and the hours preceding, is one of the most crucial times of any household with children. It might be advantageous for you to examine what takes place during this time and how it affects the tone of the home for the evening.

Your husband calls about 4:30 asking, "What's for supper tonight?" To which you reply with a creative stall technique which really means, "I haven't thought about supper yet."

Your husband will be home soon and you have to get something going. Maybe if you complain enough, he'll see the need for a microwave oven, or take the family out for dinner. Or maybe he won't see the need for either, but will criticize you for your lack of organization.

You are tired and grumpy and your children are beginning to sense your uneasiness. Their energy level seems to rise as yours diminishes. To compensate for this you begin to let everyone know how unhappy you are. Slamming a few cupboard doors and yelling at them helps vent your frustration. A general feeling of self-pity comes over you and you feel like you want to explode.

Your husband walks in not knowing what to expect. He sees

you are in a bad mood and tired, yet he doesn't offer any consolation. He is cautious, realizing that anything he says may trigger a negative response. So he buries his head in the newspaper and waits patiently for the call for dinner.

Of course, this infuriates you and you begin to pout and slam a few more cupboard doors just to let him know how you feel. Everyone feels the sharpness in the air.

How can a situation like this be changed? With a little willingness on your part to react in a manner opposite to what your human nature tells you, you can change this adverse situation into a comfortable one.

Dot, a dear friend of mine, shared with me a technique she has used to establish a tranquil atmosphere during hectic times of meal preparation. I have personally used this little technique for years and my family still allows me to get away with it. Maybe it is because they enjoy the effects it produces.

Most husbands and children enjoy coming into a home where everything is under control, especially supper. A husband loves entering his home after a hard day's work to find his wife happily moving around in the kitchen cooking a meal. Add to this an aroma which says supper is well on its way. It is a good feeling for him. He can unwind from a busy day, since his wife has everything under control.

It all sounds so ideal and we would like it to be true in our homes. But with the busy pace all of us keep, how can it take place?

Dot knew how difficult suppertime was for me, especially with the heavy schedule I kept. She also knew how things often fell apart in my home around this time. I was tired, the telephone would ring constantly, the children were fussy, and sometimes I had forgotten to take the meat out of the freezer. As a result of my poor planning, the hours of the evening which we spent together as a family were somewhat upsetting to everyone.

"Instead of becoming all unraveled about dinner, try to remain calm and happy," she said to me one day. "A lot easier said than done," I replied sharply. "How can I be calm when I have six people to feed and don't have any idea what I am going to make?"

"You have to make a conscious effort to remain calm and act as though you have everything under control. Remember, you set the tone for your home. If you are happy, the members of your family will feel this."

What a challenge! But I knew it was my only choice. I realized that I was often like a thermometer, registering what was going on around me. Sometimes I was up but many times I was down. Now it was necessary for me not to be the thermometer but the "thermostat." I was to be responsible for controlling the feeling which existed in my home.

One of the first things which Dot suggested I do was to get a pot of water boiling on the stove. To this I would add one onion. When the onion stewed, the air became filled with an aroma any nostril recognized as a meal cooking. This pot of boiling water indicated that something was in the making; therefore, my family was content. At first, they didn't catch on to my tactics, even when the pot stayed on the stove during supper. They were content in assuming that Mother was in charge and all was going well. Little did they know how fast my mind was racing to come up with something to serve them.

The next step was to defrost the meat, by chipping or cooking or both. "Remember," Dot reminded me, "the key to success is not in the pot of boiling water, or the onion cooking in it. It is in your disposition and attitude while you work."

A smiling face means Mom is happy. So despite the tenseness I felt, I smiled a lot and spoke softly, and now and then hummed a song while I worked around the kitchen. My children know that when Mom smiles and sings, all must be well with the world.

I always keep a box of Hamburger Helper on hand, just for such emergencies, and it wasn't long before supper was about ready. When the children set the table, they even included fresh flowers from the garden.

I'm not advocating that you make a practice of haphazard meal planning. Your family is important and supper should be well thought out to insure proper nutrition and a pleasant, warm experience for your family. But there are days when your weariness or lack of organization get the best of you. These are the times when just a pleasant spirit and right attitude really pay off.

My husband laughs when he finds that I am up to my old trick of boiling onions in water. But it doesn't matter. I haven't vented my frustrations on him and I have set the tone for my home. He knows how much this has paid off in the life of our family.

Defending the Home

How blessed are the children who have a happy and contented Mom; a Mom who knows and loves Jesus; a Mom who hums or sings in her kitchen, and in times of turmoil asks for God's help to quiet her troubled heart. She is the one who is able to transform any ordinary kitchen into a place where God is present as a special guest.

Proverbs 14:1 states: "A wise woman builds her house, but the foolish tears it down with her own hands."

Proverbs 24:3–4 reads: "By wisdom a house is built, and by understanding it is established; and by knowledge the rooms are filled with all precious and pleasant riches."

If we are aware of it or not, we are in the process of either constructing the walls of our homes or tearing them down with our very own hands. If resentment, bitterness, strife, an unforgiving spirit, and unkind words are part of your family's everyday experience, then the walls of your home are being torn down, inch by inch, leaving a family defenseless against the attacks of Satan.

I want to be a wall builder, using the knowledge, understanding, and wisdom found in God's Word. I want my home to be filled with the precious and pleasant riches of kindness. I desire laughter to ring from the walls and for my children to be filled with the very joy of Jesus.

It all sounds rather idealistic, especially in a society where families are struggling. God's will for the family is that they be united, and He will provide every resource available through the Holy Spirit to make this ideal possible. He has given us the choice to either build or destroy.

Psalm 127:1 is a promise of hope that I claim, because I know that my strength is not sufficient to see me through: "Unless the Lord builds the house, they labor in vain who build it."

Sometimes I fall into the trap of working so hard to be the perfect Mom, and then I wonder why it all seems so difficult and why I fall so short of perfection. I need to remember that it is the Lord who builds. He sets the foundation and then calls us to become His skilled laborers in constructing the walls. Anything which He requires of us, He will enable us to do. He will be with us, because this is His promise to us.

In the Old Testament there is an account of a very brave man by the name of Nehemiah, who led in the rebuilding of the walls of Jerusalem.

Even though Nehemiah was a captive in Persia, his heart was in Jerusalem. For news had reached him that the walls of Jerusalem were down. The people living in the city were defenseless against their hostile neighbors, and the temple which had been rebuilt by Zerubbabel some 150 years before was also vulnerable. To the Jew, a city without strong walls was really no city at all. Nehemiah could not stand the disgrace to his beloved city, and so he requested permission to return to Jerusalem and begin rebuilding the city wall.

Nehemiah's job was not going to be an easy one. Not only would there be work of enormous magnitude, but there would be opposition from people around who did not want this wall built. He was in for a battle, but he persevered.

Work continued "from dawn until the stars appeared" (Nehemiah 4:21). Criticism and persecution kept coming, causing the laborers to be fearful. Nehemiah commanded them to work with a trowel in one hand and a weapon in the other hand. The wall was finished in record time, providing security and protection for the people living in Jerusalem.

God calls us today to be mothers who build walls of protection around our children. Our homes need to be refuge places for the members of our family, filled with the light of Jesus Christ. Children growing up in such an environment are able to discern between "light and darkness." They become sensitive to other people's feelings. They know that bad language and dirty jokes are not acceptable.

There will be times when they will fall into temptation, but they will know right from wrong. They will not be deceived into believing that purposeful sinning is right, because the Holy Spirit has made their hearts and minds sensitive to the darkness of Satan.

Sad to say, most homes are battlegrounds of the devil instead of workshops of the Holy Spirit. Discontent, envy, strife, confusion, disorder, profane language, and other types of darkness are all too common.

Children growing up in an atmosphere of darkness are usually unable to distinguish between right and wrong. As a matter of fact, they frequently take the darkness of the world and satanic power to be light.

If the love of God is not present in the homelife of a child, he then searches for it outside the home. This search has taken many young people into the occult or various cults. And others as readily go along with their friends into drugs and sexual abuse, in their search for love and acceptance. One of the best ways to protect our children from the powers of darkness is to allow our homes to radiate the light of Christ.

Several years ago, my husband and I wanted to treat our children to an evening out at the movies. We scanned the paper and found a Western which was labeled PG. Without investigating what the movie was really like, we took the children. After 15 minutes, we knew we had made a mistake. The language was profane and ugly, and our children knew it. They sat with their hands over their ears. Finally, David nudged Warren and said: "Dad, I don't think we belong here. Maybe we should go."

David later told us, "Those bad words burned my ears." Our children were sensitive to things which were not pleasing to God, because they were accustomed to the light of Christ within our home.

We are in a battle to defend our homes. The very lives of our children are at stake. To keep the walls in good repair will cost us something. At times we will be building with one hand and defending with the other. We will be criticized by others. The attack of well-meaning individuals who downgrade the role of mother is constantly present. Other people may refer to us as fanatics and accuse us of brainwashing our children with religion. The pressures of time and scheduling work against the continuity of the home. The imbalanced emphasis society places on financial gain is ever present.

"Our God will fight for us" (Nehemiah 4:20) are the words Nehemiah spoke to people faced with problems similar to ours. God is the One who will, in the end, be glorified for accomplishing the task.

Whatever the condition of the walls of your home at the present time, God can work in you to begin the repair job which needs to take place. Remember that it is His will for your children to grow up in an atmosphere of His love.

With the Lord begin Thy task,
Jesus will direct it.
For His aid and counsel ask,
Jesus will perfect it.
Every morn with Jesus rise,
And when day is ended,
In His name then close thine eyes.
Be to Him commended.

(Author unknown)

10
From the Rising of the Sun

After one of my seminars on "How to Share Jesus with Your Children," a young mother challenged me, "You make it sound so easy. How is it possible to accomplish all the things you have suggested? My day is already filled to the brim with activity. For you to ask me to do one more thing makes me want to scream!"

My heart went out to her. She was finding it difficult enough to cope with the physical care of her children, and now the spiritual care seemed one more added responsibility. She was a new Christian and had not had the privilege of growing up in a Christian home. Sharing Jesus with her children was a new experience, something foreign to her daily routine. She was going to have to begin from scratch, and the idea of trying something different made her feel uncomfortable.

I could sympathize with her frustration, as I thought back to how difficult it was for me to do all the correct things to insure the proper environment for my children. Those days were not always easy, but there was a desire within my heart which prompted me to act, so that sharing Jesus became a natural part of our family's life.

I thought back to what a typical day was like for me, where four small children constantly vied for my attention. How did I meet both their physical and spiritual needs? Could I identify with the young mothers of today and the pressures which they experience?

Afternoons were to be a time of quiet in our household, but very rarely did all four children cooperate and take naps at the same time. Only on those occasional dreary days during the rainy season in New Guinea would they all bed down for an entire afternoon. The chill and dampness of the mountain air, plus the rythmic beat of the afternoon rain on our corrugated iron roof, lulled them to sleep. I treasured this time of quiet which allowed me to prepare myself for the second half of a busy day.

When the children had not napped, 5 o'clock was the magic hour when they began to take out their aggressions on me or each other. Dissatisfied with their toys, they scattered them throughout the house and then made their way to the kitchen where I was preparing supper. Their tired, whining voices was the sound I disliked the most. Yet it was an indication they needed some love and understanding. They needed to be held close and cuddled.

Time was at a premium and my patience was short. At times I reacted toward my young children with harsh words and bitterness, because of my situation and their unpleasant complaints. But there were also many times when I was able to react in a positive way. God's love operating in my life made it possible for me to radiate love instead of bitterness to my children. My heavenly Father was holding me close to Himself and soothing my anxious thoughts. My children needed this same type of security, and by God's grace I was able to convey His love to them.

In a house which looked like a disaster, with the potatoes half peeled and water boiling on the stove, I gave in and took time to minister God's love. Sitting down in the middle of my kitchen floor, I would gather all four of them onto my lap. They would cuddle close to me as I began to stroke and tickle them. I made sure to tell them how much I loved them and how much Jesus loved them. They basked in this impromptu time of loving. It didn't take very long, just a few minutes, until they were filled with contentment and security. Their fretful spirits were soothed and they were ready to go on with the business of playing. Often I would have to repeat this during the meal preparation, but every minute of loving saved me many minutes of frustration.

I always felt relieved when Warren came home. Just his presence made all the difference, and freed me to finish supper uninterrupted. I often chuckle as I recall the giant steps he would have to take, on entering the house, to carry him over the many toys lying in his path.

After greeting us each with a kiss, he would ask, "Well, how was your day?" Did he really want to hear about it, or was he just asking out of politeness? If I began to pour out to him the major events which had taken place, I could tell by his response that he really wasn't too interested. Spilled milk and skinned knees just didn't seem as earth-shattering to him as they did to me. Compared to war, poverty, and ignorance, a little boy who refused to be potty-trained or one who tore all the labels from my canned goods were amusing and supposedly a part of any mother's day.

I was exhausted at the end of a day and wondered if anything had been accomplished. The house looked a mess even though I had cleaned it. My only hope for peace and quiet was bedtime, and by then I was usually too tired to enjoy the remaining hours of solitude left in my day.

From the first crow of our boastful rooster, indicating that the sun would soon be making its appearance, to the setting of the sun over the majestic mountain range behind our home, my days were jam-packed with activity. The physical care of my children overwhelmed me. I felt like a mother grasshopper trying to keep track of her active jumping children. They wore me out, tried my patience, and tested my endurance.

Now I appreciate being young when my children were born. I had the energy and endurance necessary to make it through an exhausting day of caring for small children. It's amazing how mothers survive those early years. Yet, we really have no other choice, and we might as well make the best of the situation, using every available resource which God can give to make those years as pleasant and fruitful as possible.

A Mother's Faith

"From the rising of the sun to its setting the name of the Lord is to be praised" (Psalm 113:3). Is it possible, with our busy lifestyles, to proclaim the greatness of God from morning till night?

The Children of Israel were to faithfully teach their children the Word of God throughout the entire day. It is a command which is also to be taken seriously by us.

> And these words, which I am commanding you today, shall be on your heart; and you shall teach them diligently to your sons and shall talk of them when you sit in your house and when you walk by the way and when you lie down and when you rise up (Deuteronomy 6:6–7).

We may believe this to be true, but question how it is to take place in a home already pressured by activity.

If God asks us to do anything, He Himself will equip us to do it. He is the One who gives us the ability and provides the avenues for success (Philippians 1:6; 2:13). All He requires is a heart willing to accomplish His purpose.

It is God's will for your little children to learn of His love. Therefore, within the framework of the home, He will provide what is necessary for this to take place.

- God works with the desires in your heart. It would be worth your while to examine the desires you have for your children. What do you want to see accomplished in their lives? What are your goals in raising them?

After examining their goals for their children, many mothers find that physical well-being and gain are of prime importance. We live in a society focused on education, financial gain, and work success. We strive to make life prosperous for our children. We want them to become well-adjusted adults with an advantageous background.

Many American families are building their lives on material things, forgetting that things do not bring happiness. In the end, everything material will be destroyed. Yet many people invest a lifetime in things which really have no eternal value.

Billy Graham once said that people try to fool themselves into believing that they will be able to take it all with them. But nobody ever saw a hearse pulling a U-Haul trailer.

God has given us things to use and people to enjoy. Somehow that order has been reversed in our society—people are being used so that things can be enjoyed. Only two things on earth will last forever—people and the Word of God. All else is going to be destroyed. I want to invest my life in what has eternal value. I want to adequately invest in the lives of my children, doing everything possible to prepare them for heaven. I want to use my time with them wisely so that I may stand proudly before God at the last day. I don't want the physical care of my children to be so important that I forget about ministering to them the Good News of salvation. What would it benefit me if I gained the whole material world for them but lost them to the ravages of Satan and hell?

Teaching her children about Jesus begins first in the mother's life, as she seeks "those things which are above" (Colossians 3:1). When her heart attitude is in line with what God wants, a mother begins to see things happen in her home.

As a young mother I never thought too much about the "how

to" of sharing Jesus with my children. Few books were written on this subject. But I did have one thing in my favor—the longing in my heart to lead my children to know Jesus as their personal Lord and Saviour. I wanted to share Jesus' love with them. He was real to me and I wanted Him to be a living part of their experience too. Half the battle was won just by my willingness to do what God wanted of me. "Delight yourself in the Lord; and He will give you the desires of your heart. Commit your way to the Lord, trust also in Him and He will do it" (Psalm 37:4-5). If you have set your heart on these same things, then the Lord will enable you to teach your children God's love.

You may feel that you are handicapped by not growing up in a Christian home. Maybe you have had no model on which to pattern your Christian life. While being brought up in a Christian home is certainly an advantage, it is not a prerequisite. God works with individuals right where they are. This is His appointed time in your life. God holds the promise for today and the future is also in His hands. You are unique and He will guide you as an individual to meet the needs of your children.

• The words of Deuteronomy 6:6-7 are prefaced by this command, "And you shall love the Lord your God with all your heart and with all your soul and with all your might" (v. 5). The immense joy of sharing Jesus with your children begins with your relationship to Jesus. As you live in close daily union with Jesus, through the study of His Word and in prayer communion, seeking His kingdom and His righteousness first (Matthew 5:33), the Holy Spirit becomes your private tutor. He will teach you all things and show you how to put into practice everything you will need to know in order to lead your children to Christ (John 14:26).

When Jesus is first in your life, when you know that He died on Calvary and won eternal life for you in heaven, and when you receive Him into your life as your personal Lord and Saviour, everything else fits into its proper place (Matthew 5:33). This knowledge then prepares you to live in Christ, on a daily basis.

• As a result of faith in Jesus, you have the Holy Spirit in your life. He jealously desires control of you (James 4:5). Yielding to His control enables you to live a life which is glorifying to Jesus. This will not always be easy. We are all basically selfish, with strong desires to please ourselves. Your life constantly needs to be brought under the influence of the Holy Spirit.

As mothers, we often rebel against our role in the home. The servant heart which we need is foreign to our human nature. When we rebel, we fall into self-pity, outrage, bitterness, anger, and harsh words. The Holy Spirit wants to change all of that. He wants us to be dominated by our new nature which is formed in the likeness of Jesus Christ. He wants to produce in us the fruit of the Spirit, love, joy, peace, patience, gentleness, kindness, self-control, long-suffering, faithfulness (Galatians 5:22). Only as we surrender ourselves to His power will we be able to share Jesus with our children.

As we review the sequence of things which need to take place in our own lives before we actively share Jesus with our children, we see first, that there must be the desire; second, the personal relationship with Jesus as our Lord and Saviour; and third, the control of the Holy Spirit in our lives.

A Mother's Worship

There is no way to overestimate the importance of the example the Christian mother becomes, as she lives her life in Christ. Her performance of daily responsibilities becomes a silent vocabulary to her children which can either confirm or nullify the words which she speaks.

The words you speak to your children about Jesus are necessary, but they will have little meaning unless they are accompanied by the love of Jesus in your own life, and by a relationship of love with them through example. Long before they hear the words you speak, your children will hear what you are.

Christianity is really a matter of relationships. As you develop loving relationships with your children through your actions, they begin to form their ideas of what God's love is like. Children need this point of reference.

Long before I truly understood many of the things my mother spoke to me about Jesus, I saw them active in the way she lived. When she spoke, I listened, because her words were a continuation of her life. Her example made me want to listen.

I remember watching her pray in the morning, before her day would begin. I was fascinated as I peeked in the doorway. As she knelt at her bedroom window with her prayerbook at her side, I would watch her lips move. I often wondered what she was saying to God. I was captivated by the serious look on her face. She was in communion with God, discussing with Him some very crucial matters and she was not to be disturbed.

As a family, we witnessed answers to her prayers. When an answer would come, her favorite saying was, "God works in mysterious ways His wonders to perform."

Through the example of my father and mother, I came to know how necessary it is to worship God together in church on Sunday and on other special occasions. The only excuse for being absent from church was illness. As a child I enjoyed going to church, and felt a sense of God's presence there. My parents would not allow any foolishness during this hour of worship. We were on "holy ground," and reverence for God was of utmost importance. They taught us how to sit with hands folded, eyes straight ahead. We always wore our Sunday best, not because we wanted to put on a show for other people, but to say to God that we wanted to look nice for Him. We were taught to join in with the singing and the prayers, even if we didn't know all the words.

It was in church that I heard God speak to my heart and call me to dedicate my life to Him. After hearing a missionary speak when I was six years old, I decided that someday I would marry a minister and do missionary work. Twelve years later, I met Warren and my prayer was answered. He often teases me that he never really had a chance, because a six-year-old girl was praying for him when he was only nine.

As I look back, I can see why it was easy for me to love Jesus. I saw Him active in the lives of my parents. He was real! When He was spoken of, He was not some fantasy character or merely historical person. Rather, Jesus was Someone who lived in our house.

My mother's worship in the early morning hours transformed our home into a place where Jesus lived and loved. Often she would refer to the plaque which hung in our kitchen:

Christ is the Head of this house

The Unseen Guest at every meal.

The Silent Listener to every conversation.

As my mother's life was controlled by the Holy Spirit, she radiated Christ's love to us. And as that took place, the words she spoke had meaning. The examples she used in her teachings went deep into my heart. I had no other choice, it seemed. God's love was swirling around me, and my tender life was being nourished by the Holy Spirit. What a blessing to be surrounded by the love of Jesus. This was the kind of mom I wanted to be.

My mother would be the first one to admit that she did not do everything right. There were many times she wished she had done things differently. There were times when self-pity took hold and unkind words came out of her mouth. But this was not the norm for her life. She was a sinner who lived in the forgiveness which her Saviour offered her. And this fact made all the difference in her life and in the lives of her children.

You will never be perfect. You will make mistakes in raising your children. What you need to consider is what your children see as the norm for your life. Do they see your desire to live a holy life before God? Or do they see your desire to please yourself?

When we sin, God's love and forgiveness are present in the blood of Jesus. When we fail in being the moms that Jesus would want us to be, He is there waiting to pick us up, willing to give us a new start. I live in that forgiveness. It is the only hope I have for being the mother God wants me to be. The mistakes I have made in raising my children are evident, but they are not devastating, because God can heal. And I trust He will work for good, in spite of my shortcomings.

A Mother's Influence

Mothers have a strong ability to influence. Godly mothers have the potential of producing godly children. But the opposite is also true—ungodly mothers can produce ungodly children.

When you read of great men in history, you see how many of them mention the effect their mothers had on their lives. It is said that "The hand that rocks the cradle rules the world," and "Behind every great man there is a woman." You can influence your children either for good or for bad.

A newspaper story told of two families. One was the family of a well-known atheist. The other was the family of Jonathan Edwards, the great American preacher. They were contemporaries. The atheist married a godless wife, and from this union to the fourth generation of 1,200 descendants, there were 400 who were physical self-wrecks, 310 paupers, 150 criminals and 7 murderers—that was in an age that was considered puritanical. Jonathan Edwards married a godly woman. Of 1,394 known descendants to the fourth generation, there were 14 college professors; 100 ministers of the Gospel, missionaries, and theological teachers; more than 100 judges and lawyers; 60 physicians; 60 authors and editors—and almost every North American industry has been influenced by an offspring of Jonathan Edwards. (*Decision*, August 1981).

All of your teaching begins first by example. You cannot effectively teach things you yourself do not practice.

Your children need to know that you pray and that your communion with God in prayer is a necessary part of your daily life. Seeing my mother on her knees praying made a big impact on me. By her example she taught me that prayer is an important element in any Christian's life.

Do your children see you praying? How blessed they are if they see you taking out those quiet times during the day to come to God. Sometimes we feel self-conscious about our praying. We don't want anyone to see us and so we try to wait for quiet times.

My children would often join me as I prayed. As I knelt beside my bed with my head bowed and eyes closed, I would feel a little body kneeling next to mine. There would be Johnny or Elisabeth, not at all embarrassed, but instead joining me with their eyes so tightly closed, reciting the most recent prayer they had learned.

My favorite spot now for meeting with God is my kitchen table. Before the day begins I like to take time to ask God to be with me throughout the day, to help me live to His glory. I ask that His love will fill my home so that each child will feel the love of Jesus. What a blessed time that is for me. My home is prepared. As the members of my family rise they meet Jesus in my kitchen, because He has been there as I have prayed. It makes a difference!

Every once in a while one of them walks in before I am finished. I pray that when they see me praying, it will have the same effect on them as my mother's example had on me.

The study of God's Word is another important element your children need to see in your life. Do your children know that you place great importance on the Word of God? Is there a Bible present in your home? Do they see you reading it? As they observe your perseverance as you discipline your life to study God's Word, you are once again teaching them.

I found it difficult to block out a period of time to read the

Scriptures when my children were toddlers. They were always there wanting my undivided attention, and very few free moments existed. I found that reading the Bible out loud to my toddlers made them feel a part of what I was doing. Every opportunity I had, I would read to them. Often I would take their little fingers and point to the words as I read. Even though they could not understand the words or read for themselves, they could understand my love and the attention which they were getting. It made them feel important to be able to read along with Mom. I would always tell them how much I loved this book called the Bible, because it told me all about Jesus. I would sing to them the little song:

I'll never give up my Bible,
My beautiful, beautiful Bible,
I'll never give up my Bible,
It is so precious to me.

As I sang, I would let them hold my Bible close to their hearts, showing that they also loved God's Word. Soon they learned the song and would sing along with me.

Many Christian bookstores have little pocket Bibles for small children. They are inexpensive but precious to any little one who has learned to love and respect God's Word. As I read my Bible, they would pretend to read their little ones.

The Bible was a special book and therefore had a special place in our home. It was not to be mistreated in any way, or left on the floor or hidden under other books. Our children were told to care for their little Bibles and have a special place to keep them.

After I would read to them, I would then tell them it was important for Mommy to read quietly by herself. "Find a few toys to play with while Mommy reads. You can play with them for just a few minutes. See how quiet you can be. I'll set the timer for five minutes and when it rings you will know that I am finished." Somehow they understood. When the time was up, they knew they could resume normal activity. They began to learn that I needed this time of quiet.

As they grew older they learned to respect my time alone. Often I would go into my bedroom to read and pray, only to see four little ones outside the door waiting for me to finish.

It was said of Suzanna Wesley that she seldom had any quiet place in her home in which to pray. But her 11 children knew the signal when Mother wanted to pray. All she needed to do was lift her long white apron over her head and there was silence. This was Suzanna's prayer closet and she was not to be disturbed.

Some afternoons, when no technique would work, I would gather my children in my bed and read to them. The rainy afternoons in New Guinea were sometimes cold and damp, and all of us together under the blankets produced an atmosphere of warmth and security. As we snuggled close together, I would read them a story about Jesus. As I read, the sound of my voice would cause them to fall asleep. They felt secure in my love and at the same time were learning that I loved God's Word. It was not so important that they understood all the details. I left that up to God. It was His responsibility. His Holy Spirit was working in their lives. I was just allowing Him to use me.

Worship of God with other believers is also an important element of example which our children need to see active in our lives. It is my belief that even babies should be brought to church. Of course, if they are fussing and causing a disturbance we need to use some common sense. Children are able to learn at a young age how to sit quietly and worship God.

Even in the primitive surroundings of our New Guinean village, going to church was something special. Our bush church, with its dirt floor, woven cane walls, and grass roof, was a place set aside to worship Jesus.

Each Sunday was an opportunity to get dressed in our Sunday clothes. Our little ones were instructed to fold their hands, bow their heads, and pray. They were told that church was not a place to play but to pray and sing songs to Jesus. I have precious memories of my children trying so hard to be good. They learned the Ipili hymns far faster than I did. They would sing many times when they were not supposed to and do things which did not please me, but again, it was a process of training.

What a thrill it was for me when our youngest child finally made it through an entire church service without fussing. After seven years, I was finally able to listen to an entire sermon, undisturbed. As our children grew older, we progressed from the back row of the church to the front. I was proud. I had made it through those rough years.

Through the example of your life, you are able to teach your children the Word of God from the "rising of the sun to its setting." This type of teaching will come from your dedication to the Lord Jesus. When you allow God's Word to live in you, and His Holy Spirit to control and empower you, you will reflect the love of Jesus to your family.

11
Growing in Grace

Christians who seriously live by God's Word are in the minority. As a Christian mother in a secular society, you are in for a battle. Your ideals will not be readily accepted by others. Your commitment to motherhood and family will be challenged, and your love for Jesus may be scorned, as you try to live it out in the life of your family.

If you feel like a flickering light in the midst of darkness, you can hold to God's promise that your faith will not be extinguished. Christ is the Light of the World and His light dwells within you so that you may bring it to others. (See Matthew 5:14–16; John 1:4–5; 8:12; Isaiah 42:3.)

You may feel that you are not making an impact on the world for Christ, because you are home with little children. But the imprint you leave on your children is one of the greatest accomplishments in your life. God gives you only one time around with your children. You can never go back and do it over again. You need to use that time wisely.

The job of teaching your children begins not when they start to venture away from the home. Kindergarten is too late. It must begin before the child is even able to understand words which are spoken to him.

Pastor Larry Christenson has this to say about teaching our children:

We live in an age when 1,000 sirens beckon for the ears and minds of our children. It is not enough to teach them a code of ethics. It is not enough to teach them a few rote prayers. Our home must be so filled with the presence of Jesus that they encounter Him at every turn; come to know Him and love Him as effortlessly as they come to know their parents. In such a setting, Jesus can engage their imagination. And this is the only antidote to the powers of darkness and corruption which are loose in the world today. The time is past when parents can give their children a pleasant surface coating of religion. Our children are either going to be filled with Jesus and excited about Him, or filled with sin and excited about it. All that we can bring our children will be worthless unless we can bring them Jesus (*The Christian Family*, Bethany Fellowship, p. 166).

Anna Mow in her book *Your Child—From Birth to Rebirth* also stresses the importance of the home environment to the spiritual life of the child.

Real religion is a matter of life relationships much more than it is a matter of words. We start too late if we begin our teaching about God with words. Too many Christians have thought of God in verbal terms only. They are seemingly satisfied with the things that can be said about Him. Words are important and have their rightful place, but another foundation must come first. This foundation is built in the relationship of the home (Zondervan, p. 25).

A little boy woke during the night because of loud crashes of thunder. He was frightened and cried out to his father, "Daddy, Daddy, please come. I'm frightened."

"Don't worry," replied the father, "God loves you. He will take care of you."

"I know that, Daddy, but right now I need somebody with skin on."

As a mother you are God's love with skin on. You need to realize how important it is to be Jesus' representative of love within the home. Your children will identify more with this type of love and touch than they will with the words you speak to them, especially in the beginning stages of your teaching.

It is interesting to see how children view adults. Any adult who has a role of spiritual leadership has to be extremely careful as he deals with children. In our church the children are brought to the communion table with their parents. Even though they do not receive the Lord's Supper, they do receive a blessing from the pastor. It has happened many times that as Warren is serving Communion, the little children will wave at him, and then whisper, "Hi Jesus." Very often small children will shake hands with Warren after church and say, "See you next Sunday, God."

Because children identify God with people who are in spiritual leadership, it is extremely important that pastors, Sunday School teachers, deacons, and especially parents exhibit the qualities of Christ.

Jesus viewed children as being very important in the kingdom of God. He said, "Whoever does not receive the kingdom of God like a child shall not enter it at all" (Luke 18:15).

When children were brought to Jesus, the mothers wanted Jesus only to touch them. These mothers must have known how important the physical expression of touch was in relaying love to small children. Jesus took the children in His arms and blessed them. In doing this He was teaching them about His very nature, by loving them through His touch.

When the children were brought to Him, He didn't ask how old they were, or if they had the ability to understand. He didn't tell the disciples to organize the children in rows so that He could tell them a story. No, He took each one of them individually on His lap and loved them. He established eye contact with them. This physical touch would linger in their little minds, so that when the time came for them to be able to understand the words of Jesus, they would relate the words to the touch and would understand more fully.

You are in the process of growing Christian men and women. Your goal is to prepare them to become spiritually independent of you. In the training you provide, the discipline and love, allow the Holy Spirit to do His work in their little hearts. They are in the process of growing in grace.

We must have faith that the Holy Spirit works in even the very small child, bringing him into personal relationship with Jesus.

Missing this fundamental teaching of the Bible, we have often misconstrued our problem and responsibility as parents. On the one hand, we teach our children to sing, "Jesus loves me." Yet on the other hand, we half accept the rationalistic notion that children "can't believe," and await the day when our child will grow up and be able to "receive Christ." If only we believed the Bible, and realized how unreservedly the child *believes* when he sings! There is not the slightest thought in his heart but that Jesus indeed *does* love him. His problem is not a lack of faith, but a lack of experience. The job of the parent is to let that faith become a doorway to experience. In concrete and practical ways the parent must help the child to recognize the love of Jesus in the everyday affairs of life (Larry Christenson, *The Christian Family,* p. 151).

Just as a tiny seed planted in a garden needs lots of care to grow into a plant which will be fruitful, so your child growing in faith needs special love and care. It doesn't all happen overnight. Sometimes the process is long and tedious.

The spiritual maturation of a child's faith goes hand in hand with his physical and emotional development. As love is administered in the physical and emotional areas of a child's life, the spiritual has a secure, fertile place in which to grow.

You are preparing your children to eat "solid spiritual food" (Hebrews 5:13). Physically, babies progress from milk to solid food. For some, the period of weaning is difficult and long. Others quickly adapt to solid food.

Your children depend on you greatly for their spiritual nourishment during their early years, but eventually there comes a time when they are weaned. Instead of depending on you for that nourishment, they will encounter God on a personal basis and receive their solid food from Him, through His Word.

Each person needs this personal contact with God. So many Christians are still depending on the faith of their parents. They have never become spiritually independent. Their faith rests on the fact that they were dedicated to God at an early age, baptized, confirmed, or received into a church.

No matter how much you love your children, your faith will not save them. God has no grandchildren. Being a Christian does not automatically insure that your children will be saved. It is not the parents who do the saving of their children, but God. You are the means God provides on this earth to proclaim His saving love to your children.

When we as parents bring our babies to church to present them to the Lord, we have differing ceremonies by which we express this covenant with God, depending on the traditions and teachings of our churches. But all of us in giving our children to God fully expect His grace and faithfulness to surround and be present to them in their tender years. We believe that as we do our part of nurturing and loving, teaching and praying, God will faithfully draw them to Himself by His Holy Spirit.

This is not to say that their salvation is guaranteed, for every human has freedom of choice. But it is to say that when we stand before God with our babies, we are assured of His unending love for our children, and that He will use every means possible to draw them to Himself.

Toward Independence

In her book, *Your Child: From Birth to Rebirth,* Christian educator Anna Mow discusses the period of time before a child comes to his own experience of Christ.

> When a child has been reared in a Christian home and in a Christian church, when the temple of his mind and heart has with deep reverence been prepared for holy occupancy; the time has come when he will inevitably have his own personal encounter with the Lord of life. This encounter will not be with a stranger, for he has already learned to love Him (Zondervan, 1963, p. 135).

The day a child becomes spiritually independent of his parents is unique to each child. God is the One who causes them to be born spiritually. The time is in His hands. We cannot decide that time or hurry it along. If we would just relax, it would be a lot easier for us and our children. Instead, we become tense inside when it is not happening as fast as we want it to.

Your delightful little toddler who was once so expressive in his love for Jesus has now grown into a nonexpressive teenager. The little one who couldn't go to sleep at night without having his prayers said now becomes a 12-year-old who quietly sneaks off into his bedroom at night. He may be going through the "birthing process."

It is not easy to go through this stage of their spiritual development. I wanted to hurry the process along and "help" the Holy Spirit to cause them to make a commitment to Christ. They, of course, felt my tenseness which just delayed the process. Once I learned to relax, and to trust God that He was working within each one of them, I received a sense of peace and began to see the evidence of the Holy Spirit working. God gave me patience to wait.

We have not coerced any of our children into making a commitment. Both Warren and I have presented them with the fact that a day will come in their lives when God will deal with them as individuals. They should be open to that day.

For each of our children, their day of commitment was their confirmation. It was a day when they each came seriously before God's altar and there publicly confessed before other Christians that Jesus was their personal Lord and Saviour from sin.

What a privilege that was for me as a parent to witness. It was the natural outcome of the Holy Spirit working in their lives, bringing them each to that decision as they were growing in grace.

Just because a child is brought to this point doesn't mean that he will stop growing. The spiritual apron strings have been cut, but there still is the parental responsibility to support and nurture that child, to give wise counsel and encourage him in his faith.

Spiritual Health
In our home, we have one plant that is considered more beautiful than any other. But it was not always that way. It used to be tiny and so sick-looking that we wondered if it would ever survive.

One day when John was six, he and I were shopping in a discount store which was going out of business. We came to a table covered with small, anemic-looking plants. They were all grouped together under a sign which read, "SALE—all plants just 25¢." Since I couldn't pass up such a bargain, I let Johnny choose one plant which would be his very own. They all looked so bad I wondered if the one he picked would survive.

We adopted this little plant and took it home. We found a place for it on the windowsill above my kitchen sink. Each day

John and I would look at it, and tell it how beautiful it was. We even bought a new clay pot so it would have room to grow.

Soon the leaves began to be greener and there were more of them. After several months, the plant had outgrown its home on my windowsill, and had to be transplanted again and moved to a place where it could spread out its leaves and grow.

Now, eight years later, John's plant takes up a full corner of our living room. Everyone who sees it marvels at how beautiful it is. Needless to say, John is quite proud of it. All his years of caring have produced something admirable.

Our children are similar to this plant. They are helpless, and without Christ in their lives, they are doomed to die spiritually. But God came to rescue them from spiritual death. He bought them with a price, the sacrifice of His only Son Jesus on the cross. He knew them before they were born, before they were even thought of by us (Psalm 139:13–16). He had a purpose designed for each of their lives. He placed them in our homes, where we would love and care for them. He provided us as parents with the ability to nourish these "little plants" with His Word, with His love, as it was lived out in our lives on a daily basis.

Our little ones grew in His grace. The Holy Spirit was alive in their hearts. Different stages of growth took place and each time growth took place they were transplanted into larger pots. There, new adjustments had to be made. They needed room and freedom for new growth. The end result was the display of a healthy spiritual life which reflected the love of Jesus.

The Holy Spirit is the One who created faith within the hearts of my children. My part has been important in that I have been the instrument God has used in preparing fertile ground in the hearts of my children for the receiving of His Word for faith.

Before your babies were even born, God knew them. They are not here by accident. He has a purpose for them in His kingdom. He is giving you the opportunity to share the love of Jesus with your children. The blessings from this type of involvement in your children's lives will far outweigh any material benefits. You are leading them into a way of life which will go on forever with Jesus.

Dedicate yourself to Jesus and desire to learn from Him how to lead your children to Christ. Have faith and persevere, knowing you are in the will of God with what you desire. As you are obedient to His commands, He will direct your ways and give you success.

12
New
in the Nest

I never did like waiting rooms. And on that cold February day of 1982, the time was passing all too slowly, as I sat in the doctor's office waiting to be called. I looked around at the other women in the room. Their bulging abdomens announced their pregnant state. They looked uncomfortable and anxious, wanting to be free from the cumbersome loads they were carrying.

"Maybe the time will go faster if I read something," I thought. On the table next to me was the latest issue of *Time*, its front cover displaying the pregnant figure of a famous movie star. As I thumbed through the pages, I realized that the lead story was about the surge of older women deciding to become pregnant. Most of them are career women who have come to the conclusion that having a child later in life will bring them fulfillment.

I put down the magazine. Was I one of these women who would soon be a "mature mother"? Looking around the waiting room, I saw only young women and I just didn't fit in with them. I was 39 and had found the satisfactions of motherhood years before. I enjoyed being a mother of little children, but those days were over, and I was exploring other areas of fulfillment.

Warren had come with me to see the doctor, since he too was anxious to find out the cause of the tiredness and nausea which I was experiencing almost daily. Within the past several weeks we had discussed the possibility of my being pregnant, but somehow, it was difficult even to think about it. After all, we already had produced four healthy children well on their way to adulthood. A baby was just not logical at this time in our lives.

"Maybe you are going through an early change of life," Warren had said. "You know this is happening to women at a younger age these days." He was trying to dismiss from his mind the fact that I could be pregnant. When he realized that was of no comfort to me, his next explanation was an even better denial of my symptoms. "Maybe you have a gallbladder problem, Elise. Why not get it checked out?"

As much as I chuckled at Warren's suggestions, deep inside I too tried to avoid the thought of pregnancy. I knew it happened to other older women, but it wasn't supposed to happen to me. I chose to blame my recent hospital stay and treatment for a blood clot early in December. Maybe the emotional trauma of being bedridden for nearly a month and the medication I was taking were the reason my system was reacting as it was. Yet, all my excuses didn't fit the reality. When you have experienced four pregnancies, it is not difficult to diagnose a fifth.

"Mrs. Arndt? You can go into Room 3. The doctor will be with you in a few minutes." Warren felt my tenseness and reached over and squeezed my hand. "It's going to be all right," he said as I left. We were in this thing together and I knew that whatever the outcome, he would stand with me.

After the tests were completed the doctor came in the room and loudly announced, "Mrs. Arndt, you are pregnant. The test is positive and your uterus shows you are about nine weeks along."

The confirmation of something I didn't want to hear resounded in my mind over and over again. Was it really true? I was the mother of four teenagers and finally free from the cumbersome duties of raising small children. I had tasted freedom and was on the verge of becoming my own person. And now, I was pregnant? The reality of being drawn once again into those "desert years" was upon me—the sleepless nights, diapers, coping with a toddler.

My initial response to the doctor was, "How did this happen?" A smile came over his face as if to say, "Haven't you figured it out by now? After all, having four children should have taught you something." But he knew I needed further explanation about how modern medical science had failed and why I would be another statistic.

The smile left his face as he became very serious. "Mrs. Arndt, I need to talk to both you and your husband about the possible dangers this pregnancy may have on both you and the fetus."

A lump swelled in my throat. Never had a doctor confronted me in such a way. Telling a woman she was going to have a baby was supposed to be a joyous occasion. But as the doctor talked to Warren and me that day, I knew that it would not be the last time I would hear the words *abortion* and *amniocentesis* in relationship to this pregnancy.

My doctor of many years was a kind man, whose judgment and excellent medical knowledge we had come to respect over the years. Slowly and deliberately, he began to explain the many hazards of completing this pregnancy. Then he shared with us the options open to women in my situation. In the state of Michigan a doctor must inform a patient of any dangers to her or the fetus, and give her the choice of amniocentesis, with the possibility of abortion.

My heart pounded and tears began to well up in my eyes. Emotionally I just could not handle all that I was hearing. Warren, on the other hand, listened intently. As we heard the statistics of women my age producing children with Down's

Syndrome, Warren took my hand and held it tightly. But Down's was only a temporary concern, the doctor assured us. A simple test called amniocentesis could be performed between my 16th and 18th weeks, to determine if I would bear a Down's Syndrome child. If the test were positive, we would have the option of terminating the pregnancy.

For Warren and me amniocentesis was out of the question. What would be the use of knowing, especially if we were not planning on aborting the child? Besides, there was a 15 percent chance of endangering the fetus through this test.

My doctor then told us that the possibility of a Down's baby was not his most serious concern. Of greater magnitude was the risk of damage to the fetus as a result of medication I had been taking during the first six weeks of pregnancy. The type of blood thinner which had been prescribed is known to cause severe fetal abnormalities. There was no way to tell how much damage, if any, had taken place.

Once again my mind could not take in what I was hearing. We who had four healthy, intelligent children were faced with the possibility of producing a defective, abnormal child. Would we be able to handle or cope with such a test of our faith? How would I be able to go through seven more months of pregnancy knowing what I knew?

The days and weeks which followed were long ones, as I fluctuated between high and low. The fact that I was pregnant and had a new life developing inside of me filled me with awe. I have always loved babies, especially my own. And pregnancy, despite its discomforts, makes me feel like a walking miracle. Warren and I have not looked on our pregnancies as being a mistake, even though none of them was ever planned, and least of all this one. Our children were all conceived in love and considered as special gifts from God.

The maternal instinct which was so strong when my children were little subsided once they grew into adolescence. The business of car-pooling kids, my speaking schedule, writing, and many other activities women my age find themselves in, gave me a sense of freedom.

Yet at church when I would hold a new baby, that maternal feeling would surge inside me. People would often comment on how good I looked holding a baby in my arms. "Elise, you should have another one." To which I would reply, "It would be nice, but I'm too old for that sort of thing. A baby at 39 is fine, but a two-year-old at 41 would do me in. I'll just wait for my grandchildren; then I can spoil them all I want and send them home at night."

No longer could I talk that way. I was going to have a baby of my own. The hormones which my body was producing were causing me to feel very maternal. I was falling in love with my baby and feeling tremendous concern for the welfare of this developing person. I was filled with compassion as I thought of the struggles this little one was already experiencing, growing in my womb.

Despite the many good feelings which this pregnancy brought, there were low periods too. The thought of abortion made me sick. The possibility of my baby being dismembered, sucked out of my body, or aborted by a saline induction, caused my soul to grieve. It seemed that society at large did not care about an individual baby, mine or anyone else's. To many people, a fetus is not considered a life, created by God, but an insignificant blob to be disposed of for reasons of convenience.

I thank God for creating that love affair between me and my unborn baby in those early months. I thank Him for my Christian husband who trusted in a loving, merciful God who loved our baby and us very much. I thought of the many women in my situation who did not have this type of support.

At other times I found myself becoming depressed and feeling unsure of what was right. Did I have the option to bring a defective child into this world? A child who did not ask to be born? Was it fair to the baby? What about my own ability to cope? Would I be willing to raise a child who might need total care for the rest of his life? Was it fair to my husband? The years ahead of us were to be a time of freedom, to travel and to enjoy each other. And what about my other children? Could I expect them to understand how our life could be changed? Or about the sacrifices they would have to make?

I struggled with God in prayer. What was His will? Did He really know my situation? Did He really want this baby to be born?

All my humanness rose to the surface during those weeks. Maybe I should submit to the amniocentesis. At least we would know one way or another and then my mind could be at peace. But then, if the test came back positive, would I be tempted to seek the easy way out? Pressures to abort would come at me from others.

As I wrestled with God the answer came to me through His Word. There are no guarantees that everything will turn out the way I want. His only promise to me is that He will see us through, whatever happens.

Isaiah 43:2 does not say, If you pass through the rivers or walk through the fire. It says, When these things happen to you, I will be with you; they will not overflow you; you will not be scorched.

I knew that God's Word was the only truth that could be found on this subject, and that I had to turn a deaf ear to what the world was saying.

For Thou didst form my inward parts;
Thou didst weave me in my mother's womb.
My frame was not hidden from Thee,
When I was made in secret,
And skillfully wrought in the depths of the earth.
Thine eyes have seen my unformed substance;
And in Thy Book they were all written,

The days that were ordained for me,
When as yet there was not one of them (Psalm 139:13,
 15–16).

God knew my baby before the world was created. He knew the very time of conception, and the medication I had been taking. He knew my age, my children, and the plans Warren and I had made for the future. This fifth child was a special gift from God to our family. Who was I, with my limited knowledge and foresight, to question our infinite God?

God does not cause or will for defective babies to be born. He is not cruel, nor does He desire for us to suffer. However, it is His will for us to trust Him, to believe He is in charge of our lives. One day after struggling with God's will, I read Jeremiah 29:11, which speaks so beautifully of the sovereign will and knowledge of God: " 'For I know the plans that I have for you,' declares the Lord, 'plans for welfare and not for calamity to give you a future and a hope.' "

At this point, I began to realize that it was not the decision of abortion that I faced. I knew that was wrong. The real issue was my willingness to fully trust in God. Was I ready to trust Him for my life and for the welfare of our baby? Once more a test of my faith was at stake, a giving up of my strong will to God's will, to trust in His promise that "in all things God works for the good of those who love Him" (Romans 8:28, NIV). The real issue was trust!

God was once again teaching me about relinquishment—relinquishment of my life and also my baby's life to His purposes. I thought I had learned that lesson many times before. I knew my four children were not my own, but this child was yet unborn. Was there a difference? I do not believe so. Unnamed and not fully formed, it is still His child, His creation, someone He has planned for, before the world even existed (Ephesians 1:4).

Jesus, who has stood by me through so many other times of

struggle, has not left me alone now. He has been with me through my tears and words of anger. He has brought the peace which I have so desperately needed.

He has shown me how His own mother must have experienced many of the same feelings and turmoil which I have gone through. Her response to the news that she would become pregnant was, "Behold the bondslave of the Lord; be it done to me according to Your Word" (Luke 1:38).

When the angel appeared to her she was "greatly troubled" and afraid. The angel said to her, "Do not be afraid, Mary; for you have found favor with God" (Luke 1:30). God was going to bestow a blessing upon her which would affect the entire world. But just because she was favored did not mean that she would be exempt from sorrow. On the day of Jesus' circumcision, Simeon proclaimed to Mary that a sword would pierce even her own soul (Luke 2:35).

My response began to be that of Mary: "Behold the bondslave of the Lord; be it done to me according to Your Word." I do not understand God's ways in my life, but then I do not have to understand. My life and the life of my unborn child are in the hands of my loving Father who desires only the best for our entire family.

As peace has entered my soul and the acceptance of my situation has permeated my being, God has instructed me to dwell on the positive. The doctor with his limited knowledge is only speculating. He does not know for sure that something is wrong with my baby. He is only telling us what the medical profession knows. There is still the possibility of having a perfectly healthy child.

A Family Affair

Not long after the doctor confirmed the pregnancy, the news began to spread throughout our community and church. "Elise is pregnant!" Warren was ecstatic at the reality of becoming a father again at the age of 42. He was proud of my bulging abdomen. Many people thought it was wonderful. Few knew of the turmoil we were experiencing.

Our children, of course, could not believe that Mom and Dad had gotten themselves into such a predicament. Their initial reaction was comical. They were very honest in expressing their feelings, and we allowed them to vent their frustrations. After all, this little one seemed an "intruder" in their already settled lives.

Paul, at 17, could only think of what this would mean for him personally. He definitely was not going to give up his room. I remember his saying, "Well, there goes college and our fishing vacations. How could this happen to me?"

David, at 16, paced the floor and kept repeating, "How did this happen?" To which Warren replied, "David, you know how it happened. Should I explain it to you again?"

"Please, Dad, you don't need to explain. I know *how* it happened, but how did it happen to *you?*" He could not envision this taking place in the life of his mother and father.

Fourteen-year-old Elisabeth was delighted. Ever since my sister had had a baby, she had wanted me to produce a sister for her. Last May she approached me with the idea, to which I responded with a solid No.

"Well, if you won't have a baby on your own, then I'll have to pray for one." Little did we know that God would grant her the desire of her heart.

Johnny was delighted. He would no longer be the youngest in the family. Of course, he wanted the baby to come on his birthday the following month, forgetting it takes nine months.

They all had many questions and made it a point to tell their friends and teachers the news. It wasn't long before they began to witness the miracle of our growing baby. The movement of the arms and legs was a constant amusement. Each visit to the doctor's office stimulated much discussion about our baby. When they were able to hear the heartbeat via tape recorder, in my fifth month, they hoped to hear two heartbeats, since they all wanted twins.

For our 19th wedding anniversary, they surprised us with a designer license plate which reads "OOPS." David remembered the time a few weeks previous, when he and I were in the waiting room of the doctor's office. The woman across from me interrupted our conversation and asked if I would mind answering a question.

"Is that your son?"

"Yes," I replied.

"And you're pregnant?" came her astonished response. "Oh," she said in a dismayed tone, "this must have been an Oopsy!" David and I laughed, and from that day on our baby was nicknamed "Little Oopsy."

Family Preparations

The months have flown by and now only a few more weeks remain before the entry of our baby into its new world. Our family has had to make adjustments. We have discussed frankly with our children the possibility that this child might be born with a birth defect. We have talked over the abortion issue and are thankful that they understand that our baby and all other unborn babies are creations of God. They are willing to accept and love whatever God gives us. It has been a time for our family of drawing closer together.

My children look at other babies differently now and frequently will play with one or hold a fretful child. Often they ask me if ours will cry like that.

They look at me differently too, and have become more helpful and encouraging. One night after a LaMaze class I was telling them that I was wondering if I would make it through all the breathing techniques. David sensed that I was worried and said, "Mom, you will do fine. It's just like riding a bike. You never forget how to do it. You did it four times before. The fifth time should be a snap."

John has willingly consented to give up his room for the baby in exchange for moving in with his older brothers. They are building a room which has everything a teenager would like.

Our house is looking different these days, with a baby swing, cradle, high chair, crib, and baby clothes, all awaiting the arrival. The entire family helped decorate the baby's room.

Warren and I have made plans for the children to be present right after the birth, to see and hold their new brother or sister. This birth is truly going to be a family affair.

I was well into writing this book when I discovered I was pregnant. Most of the chapters were written from the standpoint of a mother who has been there. And now I often think about what I have already put down on paper. In the early chapters, I spoke as someone who had successfully raised four children. Now I am writing as a woman in the same situation in which many modern mothers find themselves. It was easy to write about days gone by. It is another thing to have to go through it once again and to experience the struggles.

After a period of freedom, I am now faced with the same pressures so many other women are experiencing. Money has to be a consideration, with four children soon approaching college. Will Warren and I trust in God to provide as we did during our seminary days, when we made the choice to have me stay home and care for our two babies rather than work?

Will I feel pressured to leave my baby in the care of someone else while I seek freedom and self-expression, even in serving the Lord? Somehow, it is more acceptable to do this today than it was 18 years ago.

I often wonder if I will be able to give this child the same loving nurture I gave to the other children. Will I be willing to stop what I am doing to soothe my fretful baby? Doing this takes time. I wonder if I have become too sophisticated to play "tent" with blankets covering my living room furniture. Or to allow canned goods to be strewn across my kitchen floor as my little one plays store. Will I find time to put into practice all the things I have talked about for so many years?

The world into which I am bringing our fifth child is a harsh one. I have many questions about my own abilities of coping. Yet I know the principles we used in raising our first four will be just as relevant today as they were then. Nothing has really changed. God's command to parents is still the same.

I have seen the results of raising children for Christ, of taking the profession of motherhood seriously. Every ounce of energy spent and every sacrifice made have paid off in the lives of our four teenagers. They are able to cope with the pressures surrounding them. Because Christ has been the head of our home, and Lord of our lives, they have been able to discern between good and evil.

It is normal to feel some apprehension about being a new mother again. But I also feel privileged and honored by God to have such a task before me. Once again I will have the opportunity of putting into practice the many ideals God instilled in me as a young mother. By myself it would be a difficult task, but Jesus has promised to help me. He will work with the desires of my heart and His Holy Spirit will give me the ability to carry it through. What a marvelous blessing awaits me!

Daniel Jacob Arndt
arrived
September 16, 1982.

Elise and Warren are thanking God
that Daniel is a healthy, normal baby.